Teach Yourself VISUALLY™

LinkedIn®

Lance Whitney

Visual
A Wiley Brand

Teach Yourself VISUALLY LinkedIn®

Published by
John Wiley & Sons, Inc.
10475 Crosspoint Boulevard
Indianapolis, IN 46256

www.wiley.com

Published simultaneously in Canada

Wiley publishes in a variety of print and electronic formats and by print-on-demand. Some material included with standard print versions of this book may not be included in e-books or in print-on-demand. If this book refers to media such as a CD or DVD that is not included in the version you purchased, you may download this material at http://booksupport.wiley.com. For more information about Wiley products, visit www.wiley.com.

Library of Congress Control Number is available from the Publisher.

ISBN: 978-1-118-89036-3 (pbk); ISBN: 978-1-118-89045-5 (ebk); ISBN: 978-1-118-89028-8 (ebk)

Manufactured in the United States of America

10 9 8 7 6 5 4 3 2 1

Trademark Acknowledgments

Contact Us

For general information on our other products and services please contact our Customer Care Department within the U.S. at 877-762-2974, outside the U.S. at 317-572-3993 or fax 317-572-4002.

For technical support please visit www.wiley.com/techsupport.

Sales | Contact Wiley at (877) 762-2974 or fax (317) 572-4002.

Credits

Acquisitions Editor
Aaron Black

Project Editor
Martin V. Minner

Technical Editor
Ben Schupak

Copy Editor
Gwenette Gaddis

Editorial Assistant
Claire Johnson

Project Coordinator
Patrick Redmond

About the Author

Lance Whitney is a freelance writer and reporter in the New York City area. For the past 20 years, he has written articles, columns, and reviews for a variety of technology publications and websites. He currently works for CNET as a freelance news reporter. He also teaches classes on personal technology, including one on how to use social networks such as LinkedIn.

His first book, *Windows 8 Five Minutes at a Time,* was published by John Wiley & Sons in 2012.

Throughout his varied career, Lance has worked as a writer and editor in advertising, marketing, and publishing. He also spent 10 years in the IT department at an international company where he handled everything from local technical support to global software projects.

Author's Acknowledgments

I would like to thank my acquisitions editor, Aaron Black, for trusting me to write my second book for Wiley, following the first one in 2012. I would also like to thank my project editor, Marty Minner, for his advice, wisdom, and partnership in helping me complete this book. I'd like to thank my technical editor, Ben Schupak, for all the time and labor he put in testing the many steps detailed here. And finally, I'd like to thank my copyeditor, Gwenette Gaddis, for her sharp eye and helpful feedback.

This book is dedicated to my wife Cely and to my parents.

How to Use This Book

Who This Book Is For

This book is for the reader who has never used this particular technology or software application. It is also for readers who want to expand their knowledge.

The Conventions in This Book

① Steps

This book uses a step-by-step format to guide you easily through each task. Numbered steps are actions you must do; bulleted steps clarify a point, step, or optional feature; and indented steps give you the result.

② Notes

Notes give additional information — special conditions that may occur during an operation, a situation that you want to avoid, or a cross reference to a related area of the book.

③ Icons and Buttons

Icons and buttons show you exactly what you need to click to perform a step.

④ Tips

Tips offer additional information, including warnings and shortcuts.

⑤ Bold

Bold type shows command names, options, and text or numbers you must type.

⑥ Italics

Italic type introduces and defines a new term.

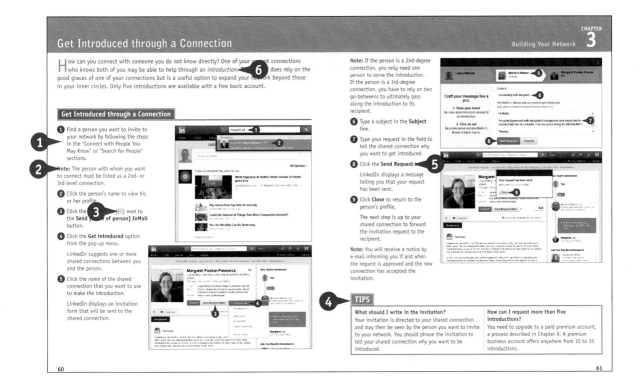

Table of Contents

Chapter 3   Building Your Network

Chapter 4   Viewing and Posting Updates

Table of Contents

Chapter 5   Communicating with Other People

Chapter 6   Revising Your Profile

Chapter 7 — Adding Endorsements and Recommendations

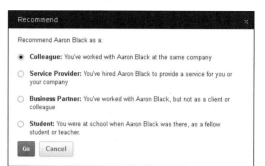

Chapter 8 — Using Groups

Table of Contents

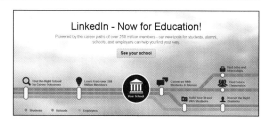

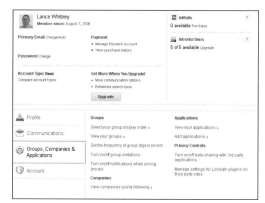

Table of Contents

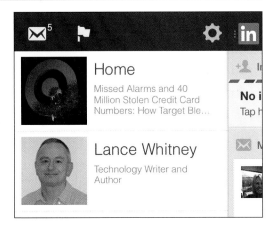

Chapter 15   Getting Help and Advice on LinkedIn

Welcome!
How can we help you?

[Search]

Popular Answers

Company Pages Products & Services Page - No Longer Supported
Applications Data Use
Managing Account Settings

CHAPTER 1

Understanding LinkedIn

What exactly is LinkedIn? Maybe you have heard of the site but have never used it, or maybe you have an account but do not fully understand what to do with it. LinkedIn is an online social network that connects you with other professionals. You can use LinkedIn to promote your job skills, find business opportunities, and exchange knowledge and advice — all with the goal of enhancing and furthering your career.

Linked **in**

Email address

Password Forgot your password?

Sign In

Join the world's largest professional network.

Get started – It's free.
Registration takes less than 2 minutes.

First name

Last name

Email address

Password (6 or more characters)

By clicking Join Now, you agree to LinkedIn's **User Agreement**, **Privacy Policy** and **Cookie Policy**

Join now

Find a colleague: First name   Last name   Search

LinkedIn member directory: a b c d e f g h i j k l m n o p q r s t u v w x y z more   Browse members by country

Set Up Your Account and Profile

Your first step on LinkedIn is to set up your account and create your profile. Think of your profile as a more in-depth and dynamic version of your resume with greater details and personal comments about your jobs, education, skills, projects, organizations, and other achievements.

Introduce Yourself with a Profile

You build your LinkedIn profile just as you might build your resume. You start off with a summary, move on to your job history, add your education, and top it off with skills, projects, and other professional accomplishments.

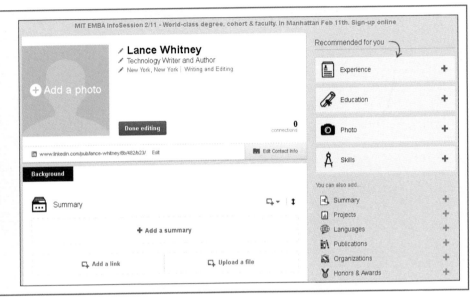

Give People a Peek at Your Photo

You can give people a peek at yourself by adding a photo to your profile. Not all LinkedIn members display a photo, but including one helps to personalize your profile.

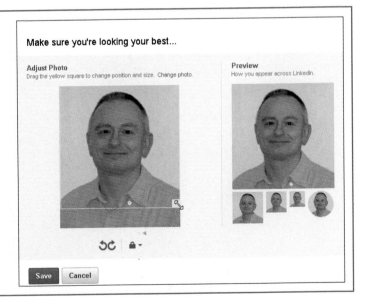

Add Your Contact Info

Beyond your e-mail address, you may want to add other ways for your LinkedIn connections to contact you, such as your phone number, instant messaging handle, and business address. Have a Twitter account? You can also add your Twitter ID.

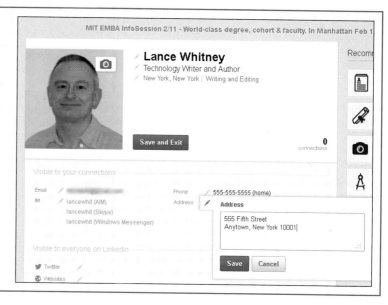

Add Your Own Websites to Your Profile

You can spice up your profile with links to your blogs, your online portfolio, your company web pages, and other websites. Adding such links easily leads people to some of your work and accomplishments.

Add Even More Details

You can add even more details to flesh out your profile — honors and awards, test scores, courses, patents, certifications, and much more.

Build Your Network

After you set up your profile, the next step is to build connections with co-workers, employers, employees, classmates, and other fellow LinkedIn members. The idea is to create a mutually beneficial network of people with whom you can share job opportunities, career advice, and other items of interest. You can invite people to connect with you, as well as accept invitations from others.

Add Contacts from Your E-Mail

One spot to look for possible connections is in your own e-mail. You can tap into your address books from Gmail, Yahoo!, and other online e-mail services.

Accept an Invitation

You can make a new connection on LinkedIn by accepting an invitation from someone else via e-mail. You can automatically accept the invitation from the e-mail or view the person's profile first to decide whether you want to accept.

Connect with People You May Know

To help you build your network, LinkedIn steers you to people you may know based on your employers, schools, and current connections.

Search for People

How do you connect with a specific person on LinkedIn? The site offers its own built-in search through which you can find people to add to your network. You can search for people by name, company, title, location, and other attributes.

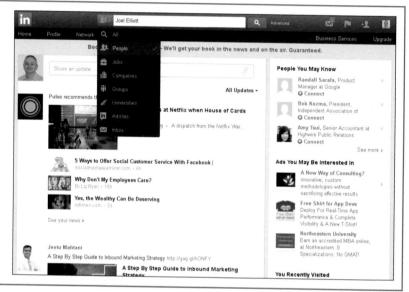

Get Introduced through a Connection

How can you connect with someone on LinkedIn whom you do not know directly? One of your current connections who knows both of you may be able to help through an introduction. This option is a good way to expand your network beyond those in your inner circle.

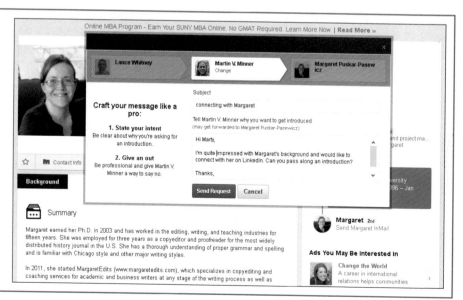

View and Post Updates

You can view updates from your LinkedIn connections to stay abreast of their professional activities. But these updates also can provide advice, comments, and articles relevant to your career and industry. You can respond to such posts and also post your own updates to share news about you, your company, and other professional interests.

View Updates from Your Connections

Your LinkedIn home page displays the latest updates from the people in your network, as well as those from sponsored companies. Many of these updates are worth reading because they offer news, analysis, and opinions on topics of value to you in your career.

Respond to an Update

Want to add your own two cents to a particular update? You can respond to an update by commenting on it, as well as by sharing it with the people in your network. Your comment may then elicit a response from the person who posted the update and from other people who read it, triggering an ongoing conversation.

Post Your Own Updates

You can share information about yourself, your career, and your company by posting an update with the latest details. But you can also share news, advice, and general information that you think would interest the people in your network.

Delete One of Your Updates

Oops, you made a mistake with one of your updates and want to delete it. No problem. You can remove an update so it is no longer visible to your connections. Keep in mind, however, that people may have already read it. But better late than never.

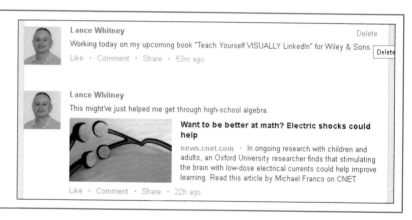

See Who's Viewed Your Recent Updates

Want to find out how many people are actually reading your updates? LinkedIn can share that information with you. You can see how many people have viewed, liked, and commented on your most recent updates.

Communicate with Other Members

After you set up your network, you can stay in touch with your connections through private e-mail. LinkedIn also keeps track of your incoming and outgoing messages so you can easily view and manage them.

E-Mail a Connection

Need to contact one of your connections about something private? You can do that through LinkedIn's own e-mail. You can view a list of all your connections at LinkedIn's contact page. From there, you can easily select the person you want to e-mail and then compose and send your message.

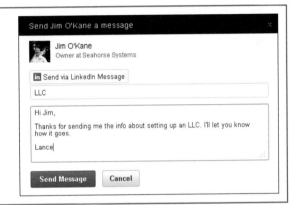

Check for New E-Mails

Any e-mail sent to you on LinkedIn is automatically passed along through your regular e-mail account. So you can easily find new messages from your LinkedIn connections in your primary e-mail. You can also check for new e-mail right from LinkedIn as well.

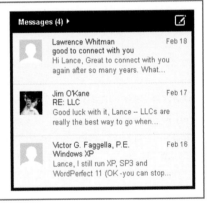

Respond to an E-Mail

You can respond to a new e-mail either from your own e-mail account or from your LinkedIn e-mail inbox. You can also read and respond to older e-mail messages by viewing them from your LinkedIn inbox.

Manage Individual E-Mails

What do you do with a new LinkedIn e-mail that you have already read? You can easily delete it or archive it. You can also delete, archive, and forward older e-mails from your LinkedIn inbox.

Search Your Inbox for Specific Messages

You need to find a specific e-mail but are having trouble tracking it down. No problem. You can search for specific messages within your entire inbox based on names, titles, companies, and other keywords.

Use LinkedIn Groups

LinkedIn offers virtual groups that you can join to network with other people who share your professional interests, skills, and industry. In a group, you can ask and answer questions and read comments from fellow members, all of which could prove helpful in your professional growth.

Find a Group

Your first step is to find a group that interests you. You can search for specific groups based on job title, industry, or other keywords.

Join a Group

When you find a group that interests you, the next step is to join it. In some groups, a manager must first approve your request to join. In other groups, your membership becomes immediate as soon as you join.

Post a Comment or Question

As a group member, you can ask questions and post comments about subjects related to that group. Asking a question taps into the collective knowledge of your fellow group members. Posting a comment returns the favor by sharing your own knowledge or advice with fellow members.

Respond to a Comment or Question

You can also contribute to a group by responding to questions and comments from other people. You can build your reputation by answering questions posted by your fellow members. Or you can simply add to the discussion by offering your reaction to another person's comment.

Create a Group

Having trouble finding a group to meet a specific niche? You can start your own group. Creating and maintaining your own LinkedIn group does require time and effort. But starting a group can be a useful way to network with people and further enhance your reputation on LinkedIn.

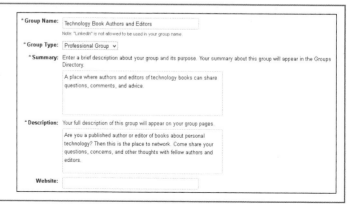

Use LinkedIn for Jobs and Business

LinkedIn can help you find your next job or business opportunity by pointing you directly to open positions and connecting you with the right people. Those of you who want to promote your own companies can use LinkedIn to attract prospective clients, customers, and employees.

Find and Follow Companies

One way to learn about potential employers is to follow them on LinkedIn. By following a company, you can see its latest LinkedIn updates and discussions at your LinkedIn home page. You may also want to follow your own employer's LinkedIn page to stay current on its latest activities.

Search for Jobs

LinkedIn's main goal is to connect you with other professionals. But the site can also connect you with specific jobs. LinkedIn offers a Jobs page where you can search for positions based on industry, location, and other attributes.

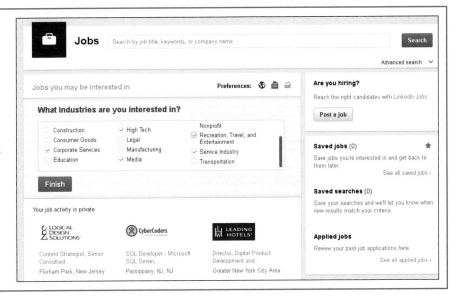

Follow News and Influencers

One way to stay in touch with the business world is through LinkedIn Pulse. The Pulse feature provides news stories based on categories such as accounting, finance, and technology. LinkedIn also provides a publishing forum through which business leaders and other influencers can write stories and columns of value to fellow members.

Post a Job

Employers can use LinkedIn to post jobs and reach out to prospective candidates. You may find it an effective way of attracting the right talent. And you can learn a great deal about a job applicant directly through that person's LinkedIn profile.

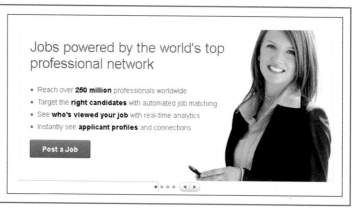

Build a Company Page

To fully promote your business, you may want to create a company page. Through such a page, you can publicize your organization, market your products and services, and advertise job openings. You can also post updates about your business to share the latest news and spark conversations among people who follow your page.

Companies Home   Following (9)

Add a Company

Company Pages offer public information about each company on LinkedIn. To add a Company Page, please enter the company name and your email address at this company. Only current employees are eligible to create a Company Page.

Company name:

Lance Whitney LLC

Your email address at company:

☑ I verify that I am the official representative of this company and have the right to act on behalf of my company in the creation of this page.

Continue or Cancel

Use LinkedIn for Education

LinkedIn is primarily a tool for professional career networking. But the site also serves a role in the world of education. Alumni can use LinkedIn to keep track of their own universities. High-school students and people who plan to resume or continue their education can use the site to research potential schools. And colleges can market themselves through dedicated pages on LinkedIn.

Use LinkedIn as a Prospective Student

Are you a current student looking to go to college or graduate school or a working professional who wants to return to school? Either way, LinkedIn can help. You can find and research schools based on your field of study, location, and other factors. You can learn about different universities throughout the world by visiting their pages, asking questions, and connecting with students and alumni.

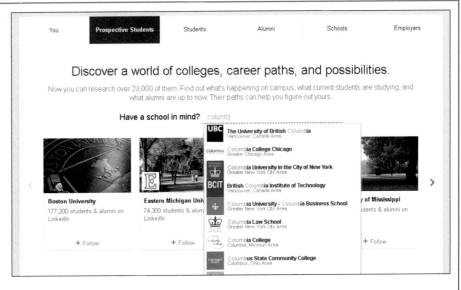

Use LinkedIn as a Student

College students can use LinkedIn to follow their schools and to search the job market. Your university's LinkedIn page will keep you up to date on the latest activities, updates, and other information about your school. And employers who use LinkedIn can lead you to entry-level jobs and internships.

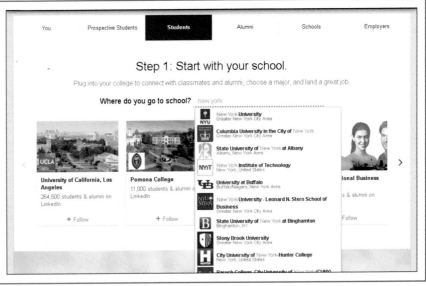

Use LinkedIn as an Alumnus

Those of you who are graduates of a university can use LinkedIn to follow your school and connect with fellow alumni. Former classmates can be a good resource if you are looking to hire someone or searching for professional opportunities for yourself.

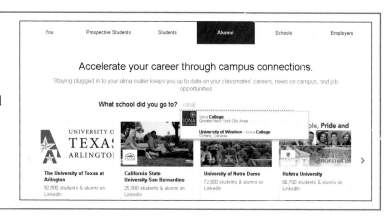

Use LinkedIn as a School Administrator

College administrators can use LinkedIn to promote their schools and attract prospective students. Using dedicated University Pages, you can share general information about your school, post updates, and highlight prominent alumni.

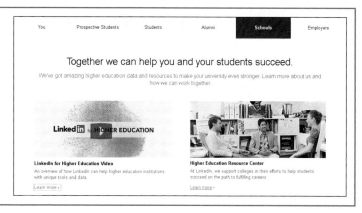

Use LinkedIn as an Employer

Employers can use LinkedIn's educational pages and services to find the right talent among students. You can set up career pages to showcase opportunities for students and create ads for entry-level jobs and internships.

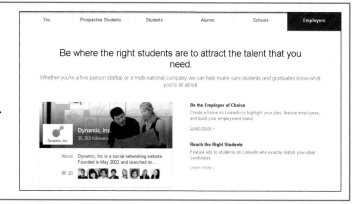

Use LinkedIn on a Mobile Device

Yes, you can access LinkedIn on the go. Whether you own an iPhone, iPad, or Android device, you can tap into LinkedIn's dedicated mobile app and specific apps for contacts and news items. You can also access LinkedIn through your device's mobile browser if no app is available.

Use LinkedIn's iPhone or iPad App

iPhone and iPad users can download and use LinkedIn's dedicated mobile apps. These apps offer a small subset of the features available on the full website. But they do give you the ability to post items, view your e-mail, make new connections, run searches, and access groups.

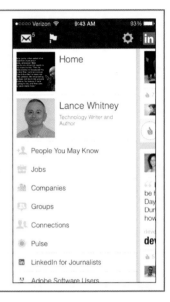

Use LinkedIn's Android App

Android phone or tablet owners can also tap into LinkedIn through a dedicated mobile app. You can use the app to access all your LinkedIn information and to update your profile.

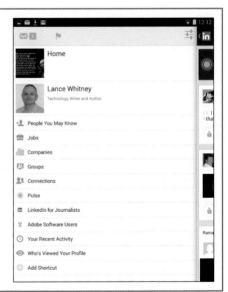

18

Use LinkedIn's Mobile Website

Own a mobile phone or tablet that doesn't have its own dedicated LinkedIn app? No problem. You can still access LinkedIn's website through your device's mobile browser. Depending on your device, LinkedIn appears either as the full site just the way it appears on your computer, or as a mobile site designed for a phone or tablet.

Use the LinkedIn Contacts App

LinkedIn Contacts is an app that helps you manage and keep in touch with all your contacts, not just those on LinkedIn. You can import contacts from other sources, read the profile information of LinkedIn members, and view alerts on their job changes and other notable events. You can also communicate with your contacts via e-mail, text message, or phone.

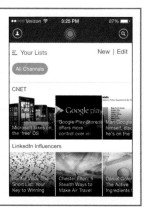

Use the LinkedIn Pulse App

LinkedIn Pulse is a dedicated mobile app for LinkedIn's Pulse feature, which offers news stories and other items of interest. The Pulse app is a news reader that serves up all the latest news items from your favorite categories in one single mobile spot. The app is available for the iPhone, iPad, and Android devices.

CHAPTER 2

Setting Up Your Account

You start off with LinkedIn by setting up a new *account* which you register with your name and e-mail address. You then create a *profile* to highlight your professional history. Think of your profile as a more in-depth and dynamic version of your resume with greater details on your jobs, education, skills, projects, organizations, and other achievements.

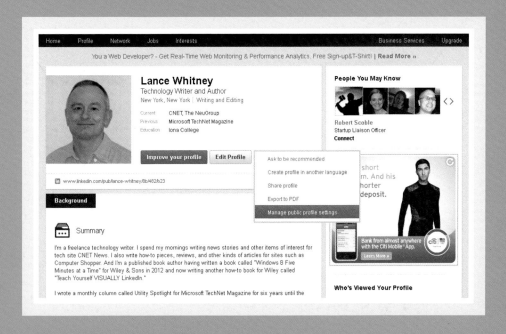

Create an Account

You create a LinkedIn account by signing up with your name and e-mail address and devising a password. You then add some preliminary details, such as your location, current job title, company, and industry.

Create an Account

1 Launch your browser, and type **www.linkedin.com** in the address bar to visit the LinkedIn website.

2 At the Get Started page, type your first name, last name, e-mail address, and a password in the appropriate fields.

3 Click the **Join now** button.

LinkedIn displays a "let's start creating your professional profile" page.

4 Confirm or change your country.

5 Type your ZIP Code in the **ZIP Code** field.

6 Click the option (○ changes to ◉) for your current status: **Employed, Job Seeker,** or **Student.**

7 Type your current job title in the **Job title** field.

8 Start typing your current company in the **Company** field, or click the **I am self-employed** option (☐ changes to ☑) if you work for yourself.

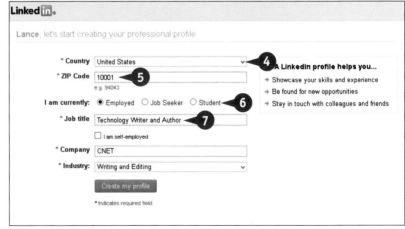

Clicking this option removes the **Company** field.

Note: After you type the first character of your company name, LinkedIn displays a list of companies that start with that letter. Continue typing, and LinkedIn narrows the list.

9 Select your company from LinkedIn's list if it appears. Otherwise, continue typing the name of your company.

10 Click the down arrow for the **Industry** field (⌄), and select your industry from the list.

11 Click the **Create my profile** button.

LinkedIn displays a "Grow your network on LinkedIn" page.

12 Check your e-mail address to make sure it's correct. But click the **Skip this step** link.

LinkedIn displays a message asking if you want to skip seeing who you already know.

13 Click the **Skip** button.

LinkedIn asks you to confirm your e-mail address.

14 If you use web-based mail such as Gmail or Yahoo!, click the button to confirm.

15 If you use an e-mail client such as Microsoft Outlook, click the link to **Send a confirmation e-mail instead.**

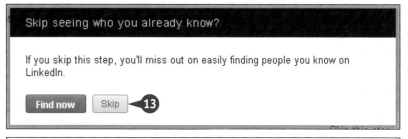

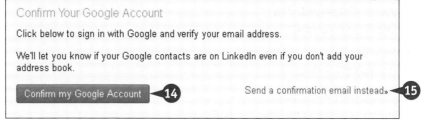

After you tell LinkedIn to send you a message to confirm your email address, you need to open your e-mail account to view that message.

Create an Account (continued)

16 Open your e-mail page or program, and look for LinkedIn's confirmation message.

17 Select the confirmation message in your inbox, and click the button to **Confirm your e-mail address.**

LinkedIn confirms your e-mail address and returns you to the "Grow your network on LinkedIn" page.

18 Click the **Skip this step** link.

LinkedIn again displays a message asking if you want to skip seeing who you already know.

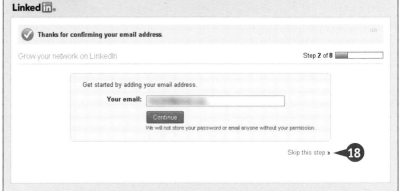

19 Click the **Skip** button.

LinkedIn displays a "Do You Know These People?" page.

20 Click the **Skip this step** link.

LinkedIn displays a page inviting you to get the app for every device you carry.

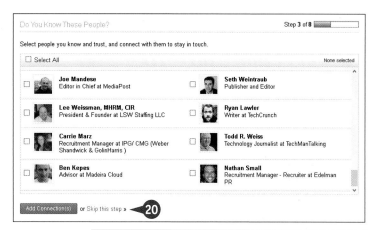

21 Click the **Skip** button.

LinkedIn displays a page asking you to choose between a free basic account and a premium account.

22 Click the **Basic Account** button.

LinkedIn displays your profile page. You can now create your profile, a topic covered in the rest of this chapter.

Note: You can close the tab or window for your e-mail account if it is still open in your browser.

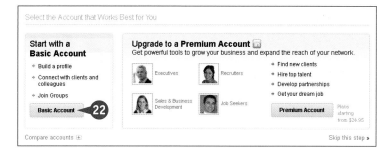

TIP

Why should I opt for a free account over a paid account?
A free account gives you the ability to try out LinkedIn's basic features. You can always upgrade to a premium paid account if you feel you want more features.

Set Up Your Profile

After you set up your account and basic details, you create your profile. LinkedIn offers a step-by-step process to build your profile by asking you a series of questions. But the order in which the questions appear varies and limits the way in which you can create your profile. Instead, you may find it more effective to build your profile manually to better control the process.

Set Up Your Profile

1 After your account is set up, LinkedIn opens your profile page and displays a blue box at the top of the page, asking you a specific question.

To turn off the questions or to set up your profile manually from the start, click the **X** in the upper right of the question box (▣) to close it.

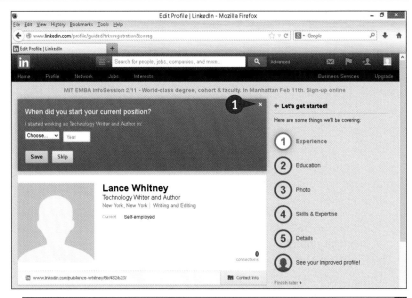

2 Click the **Profile** menu at the top of the page.

Your profile again appears.

3 Click the **Edit Profile** button.

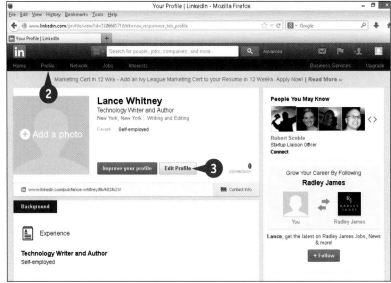

④ Review the "Recommended for you" list of profile categories.

You can use these categories to create your profile in a certain order.

Click a category, and LinkedIn moves you to that specific category.

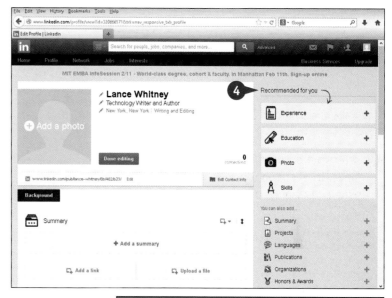

⑤ Type or select the appropriate settings to add information to that category.

But you can also get started by manually building your profile from the top on down by following the steps in the rest of the sections in this chapter.

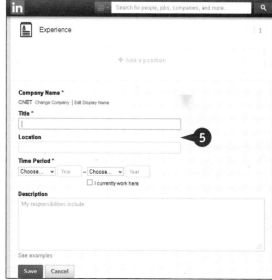

TIP

Why would I create my profile manually instead of answering LinkedIn's questions?
LinkedIn's questions force you to create your profile in a specific way. Creating your profile manually gives you more control over which sections you build and in which order you build them.

Add Your Photo

One of the first items you may want to add to your profile is a photo of yourself. Some people prefer not to add a photo, but including one will help personalize your profile. Before you tackle this step, make sure you have a suitable photo of yourself available on your computer.

Add Your Photo

1 Click the **Add a Photo** button.

LinkedIn displays the Edit Photo window.

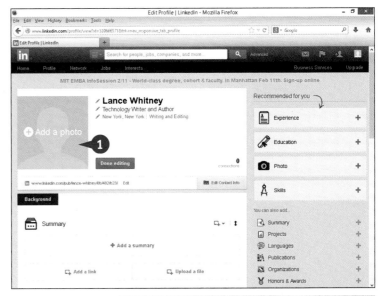

2 Click the **Browse** button.

LinkedIn displays the File Upload window.

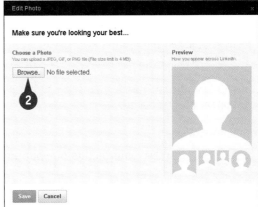

3 Browse to and double-click the photo you want to use.

Note: The image must be a JPG, GIF, or PNG file and no larger than 4 megabytes in size.

LinkedIn displays the image in the Edit Photo window.

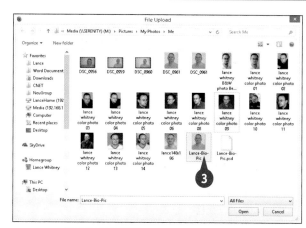

4 In the Edit Photo window, drag the yellow block in the lower-right corner of the large yellow square diagonally to resize the image.

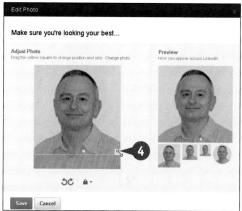

5 After you have resized the image, move your cursor to the center of the large square. Click and hold your mouse button to move your cursor to position the image.

The Preview window shows how the image will appear on LinkedIn.

6 Click **Save.**

LinkedIn displays your picture on your profile.

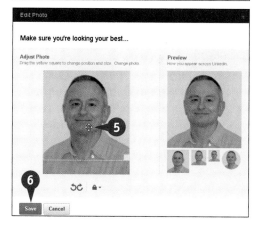

TIP

What kind of photo should I choose?
Choose a professional but friendly headshot of yourself for your photo.

Add Your Contact Info

You already added your e-mail address when you set up your account. But you may want to add other ways for people to contact you, including your phone number, IM handle, and business address. If you have a Twitter account, you can also add your Twitter ID.

Add Your Contact Info

1 Click the **Edit Contact Info** link on your profile page.

2 Click the pencil icon (✐) next to **IM.**

LinkedIn displays an IM window in which you can enter up to three IM handles.

3 Click the down arrow (▾) in the first row, and select your IM provider, such as **AIM, Skype,** or **Yahoo! Messenger.**

4 In the field to the right, type your IM handle.

Repeat steps 3 and 4 to add more entries if needed, and click **Save.**

5 To add your phone number, click the pencil icon (✐) next to **Phone.**

6 Type your phone number, and specify whether it is a **home, work,** or **mobile** number. Click **Save.**

7 To add your business address, click the pencil icon (✐) next to **Address** and type your business address. Click **Save.**

8 To add your Twitter handle, click the pencil icon (✐) next to **Twitter.**

If LinkedIn prompts you for your password, type it, and click **Sign In.**

LinkedIn displays a box to manage your Twitter settings.

9 Click the **Add your Twitter account** link.

LinkedIn displays a Twitter window asking if you want to authorize LinkedIn to use your account.

10 Click the **Authorize app** button.

LinkedIn returns to the Manage your Twitter settings box.

11 Click the **Save changes** button.

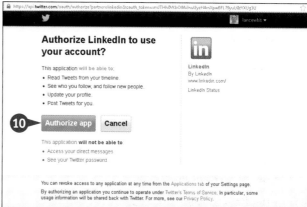

12 Click the **Profile** menu, and then click the **Contact Info** link to see your Twitter handle displayed.

TIP

What happens if I add my phone number to my LinkedIn profile?
By default your phone number would be visible to everyone, including other LinkedIn members and non-members who find your profile page via the Internet.

Add Websites to Your Profile

You can add links to blogs, online portfolios, your company web pages, and other websites to your profile. Adding such websites serves to highlight your work and accomplishments. You can add the names and URLs for as many as three websites.

Add Websites to Your Profile

1 From your profile page, click the **Edit Profile** button to return to edit mode.

2 Click the **Edit Contact Info** link to open that section.

3 Click the pencil icon (✐) next to **Websites**.

Here you can enter up to three websites.

4 Click the down arrow (⌄) for the first entry.

5 From the pop-up list, select the appropriate category for the page — **Personal Website, Company Website, Blog, RSS Feed, Portfolio,** or **Other.**

6 In field to the right, type the URL of the site.

Note: If you choose the **Other** category, you also must enter a title for the site.

7 Repeat steps **3** through **5** to add more entries.

8 Click **Save.**

9 Click the link for each site that you added to make sure the site opens properly.

10 Click the **Edit Contact Info** link to close the Contact Info section.

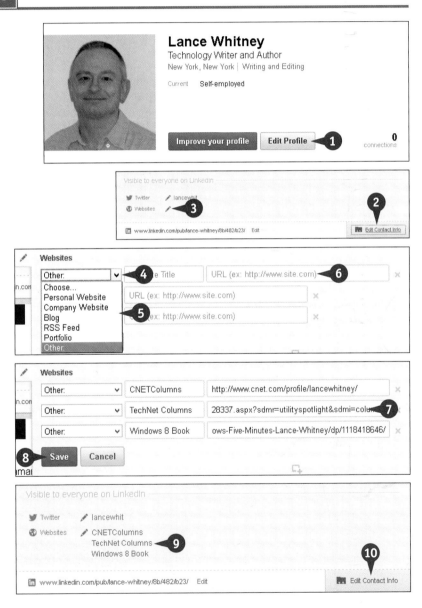

Add Your Summary

You should add a *summary* to your profile. Think of the summary for your LinkedIn profile as similar to the summary for your resume. The summary is a way to briefly describe who you are professionally and what skills you offer.

Add Your Summary

1 Make sure you are in Edit Profile mode as described in the "Set Up Your Profile" section. In the Summary section, click the **Add a summary** link.

LinkedIn displays the summary field.

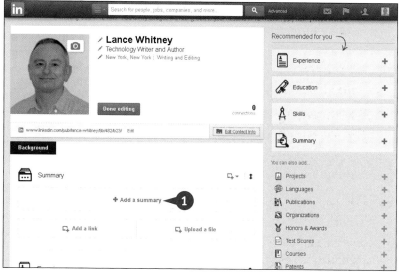

2 Type your summary in the **Summary** field.

Note: In writing your summary, try to be descriptive and specific. You have space to write several lengthy paragraphs, but do not make your summary excessively long.

3 Click **Save**.

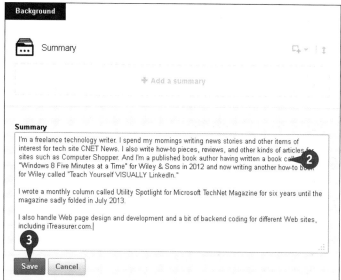

Add Your Experience

You already set up your current or latest position when you created your LinkedIn account. At this point, you can change certain information about that job and add more details, such as the location of the company, the dates you worked there, and a description of your responsibilities. You can then add any previous jobs to your profile.

Add Your Experience

1 Make sure you are in Edit Profile mode as described in the "Set Up Your Profile" section. Click the **Edit** link next to your current or previous position.

2 Confirm the company. If you need to change the name, click the **Change Company** link and type the correct company name.

After you type the first character of the name, LinkedIn displays a list of companies that start with that letter. Continue typing, and LinkedIn narrows the list.

3 Select the company from LinkedIn's list if it appears. Otherwise, continue typing the name of the company.

4 If you selected a company name from LinkedIn's list but want to change the display name, click the **Edit Display Name** link and type the name you want.

5 Start typing the location of the company in the **Location** field.

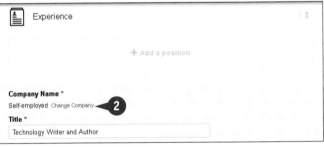

After you type the first character of the location, LinkedIn displays a list of countries, cities, and other locations that start with that letter. Continue typing, and LinkedIn narrows the list.

⑥ Select the location from LinkedIn's list if it appears. Otherwise, continue typing the location.

⑦ Select the month and type the year you started the job in the **Time Period** section. Note that the **I currently work here** box (☑) is automatically checked.

⑧ Type a description of your job in the **Description** field.

⑨ Click **Save.**

⑩ To add another position, click the **Add a Position** link.

⑪ Complete the fields for the additional position.

⑫ Click **Save.**

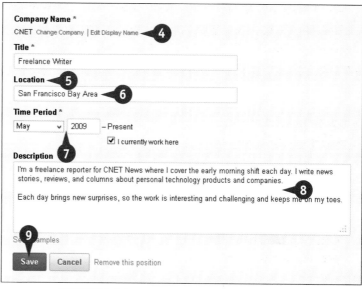

Company Name *
CNET Change Company | Edit Display Name ◄ ④

Title *
Freelance Writer

Location ◄ ⑤
San Francisco Bay Area ◄ ⑥

Time Period *
May ▾   2009   – Present
☑ I currently work here

Description ⑦
I'm a freelance reporter for CNET News where I cover the early morning shift each day. I write news stories, reviews, and columns about personal technology products and companies.

Each day brings new surprises, so the work is interesting and challenging and keeps me on my toes. ⑧

See Samples

Save   Cancel   Remove this position

📄 Experience   ↕

➕ Add a position ◄ ⑩

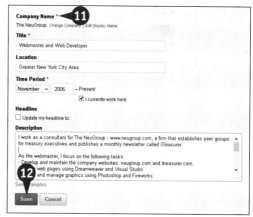

Company Name * ◄ ⑪
The NeuGroup Change Company | Edit Display Name
Title *
Webmaster and Web Developer
Location
Greater New York City Area
Time Period *
November ▾ 2006   – Present
☑ I currently work here

Headline
☐ Update my headline to:

Description
I work as a consultant for The NeuGroup - www.neugroup.com, a firm that establishes peer groups for treasury executives and publishes a monthly newsletter called iTreasurer.

As the webmaster, I focus on the following tasks:
- Develop and maintain the company websites: neugroup.com and itreasurer.com.
⑫ web pages using Dreamweaver and Visual Studio
and manage graphics using Photoshop and Fireworks.

See Samples

Save   Cancel

TIP

How should I list my experience if I am self-employed?
If you are self-employed, you may want to list each of your major clients and long-term projects as separate jobs.

Add Your Education

Your can next add your educational background to your profile. Start by adding your most recent or current school, such as a college or university, and then add your high school if needed. You can also add vocational schools or any other educational programs that you have taken.

Add Your Education

1 Make sure you are in Edit Profile mode. Click the **Add education** link.

2 Start typing the name of your school in the **School** field. Select your school from LinkedIn's list if it appears. Otherwise, continue typing the name of your school.

3 Click the arrows under **Dates Attended** ([⌄]), and enter the start and end years (or expected graduation year).

4 Start typing your degree in the **Degree** field. Select your degree from LinkedIn's list if it appears. Otherwise, continue typing the name of your degree.

5 Start typing your concentration in the **Field of Study** field. Select your study field from LinkedIn's list if it appears. Otherwise, continue typing the name of your field.

6 Type your final grade in the **Grade** field.

7 Type the names of any extracurricular activities in the **Activities and Societies** field.

8 Type a description of your studies in the **Description** field.

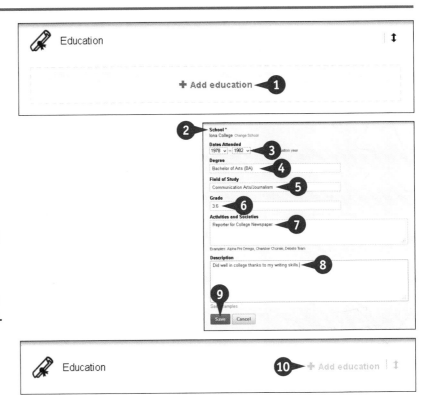

Note: Click the See Examples link to view ideas for a description.

9 Click **Save.**

10 Repeat steps 2 to 9 to add another school.

Add Additional Info

You can add additional information to spruce up and personalize your profile. You can include such items as personal or professional interests, personal details, and advice on how people can contact you and what type of opportunities interest you.

Add Additional Info

1 Make sure you are in Edit Profile mode. Scroll down to the **Additional Info** section.

2 Click the **Edit** link next to **Interests.**

3 Type any interests that you want to add to your profile, and click **Save.**

4 Click the **Edit** link next to **Personal Details.**

5 Click the down arrows for the month, date, and year of your birth ([∨]) to select the appropriate dates.

6 Click the down arrow for **Marital Status** ([∨]) to select **Single** or **Married.** Click **Save.**

7 Click the **Edit** link next to **Advice for Contacting (your name).**

Type some details on your availability and/or the type of opportunities you seek, and click **Save.**

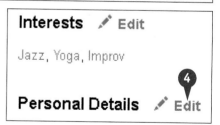

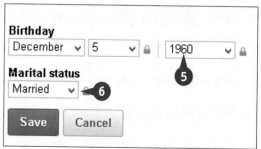

Add Your Skills

You can list your various *skills* to highlight specific areas of expertise. You can add a general skill, such as writing, and more specific skills, such as Speech Writing or Creative Writing. You can add as many as 50 different skills to enhance your profile.

Add Your Skills

1 Make sure you are in Edit Profile mode. Scroll down to the Skills & Endorsements section.

2 Click the **Add skills** link.

3 In the **What are your areas of expertise?** field, start typing the name of a skill you want to add.

After you type the first character of your skill, LinkedIn displays a list of skills. Continue typing, and LinkedIn narrows the list.

4 Select your skill from LinkedIn's list if it appears. Otherwise, continue typing the name of your skill, and click the **Add** button to add the skill.

5 Repeat steps **4** and **5** to add more skills.

Each successive skill appears in your profile.

Note: After you have added all your skills, you can reorder them by dragging and dropping a skill name to another position.

6 Click **Save**.

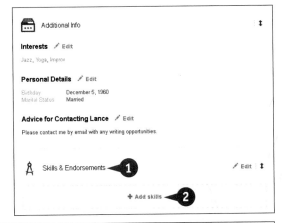

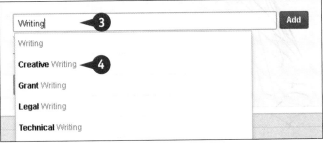

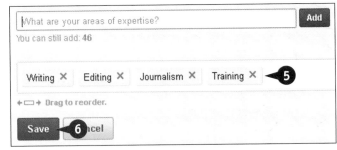

Add Your Projects

You can further enhance your profile by adding details on any projects that you have worked on professionally. These can be ongoing or current projects or ones that you have worked on in the past. They also can be projects associated with one of your jobs or those that you worked on outside of one of your employers.

Add Your Projects

1 Make sure you are in Edit Profile mode. Scroll to the top of your profile page, and click the **Projects** box.

2 Type the name of the project in the **Name** field.

3 Click the down arrow for the **Occupation** field (⌄), and select the job associated with this project, or set the choice to **Other** if the project is not associated with a specific job.

4 Click the month and year arrows in the **Date Range** field (⌄) to select the month and year.

5 If the project is ongoing, click the **Switch to date range** link (see inset).

6 Type a web address associated with this project, if one exists, in the **Project URL** field.

7 Type the names of any other people involved in the project in the **Team member** field.

8 Type a description of the project in the **Description** field.

9 Click **Save**.

10 Click the **Add** link in the Projects section and repeat steps **3** through **9** to add more projects. Click **Save**.

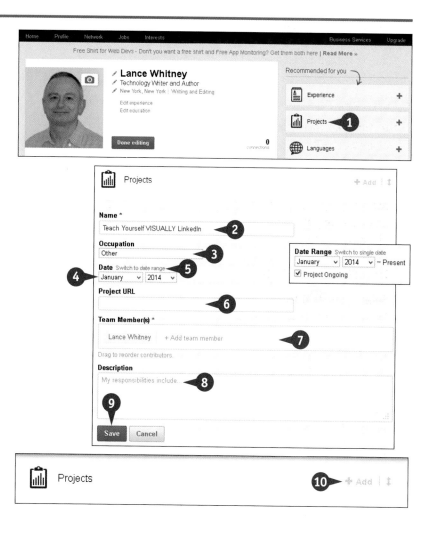

Add Your Organizations

Are you a member of any professional groups or organizations? If so, you should add that information to your profile. These can be organizations associated with one of your specific jobs or just external groups related to your career or professional interests.

Add Your Organizations

1 Make sure you are in Edit Profile mode. Scroll to the top of your profile page, and click the **Organizations** box in the right column.

LinkedIn adds an Organizations section to your profile and moves you to that section.

2 Type the name of the organization in the **Organization** field.

3 Type your position in the organization in the **Position(s) Held** field.

4 Click the down arrow for the **Occupation** field (⊡), and select a job with which the organization is associated. If the organization is not associated with a particular job, bypass this field or choose **Other.**

5 Click the month and year arrows (⊡) to select the month and year that you joined this organization.

6 If you are no longer a member of the organization, check off the **Membership ongoing** option (☑ changes to ☐) and select the month and date that you left the organization.

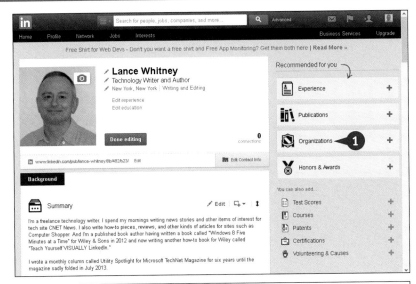

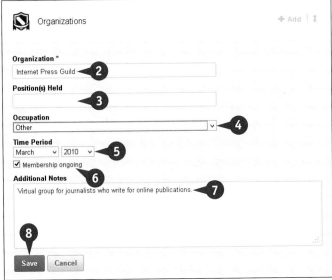

7 Type a description or notes about the organization in the **Additional Notes** field.

8 Click **Save.**

9 Click the **Add** link in the Organizations section and repeat steps 3 to 8 to add more organizations.

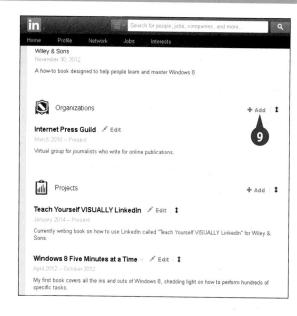

TIP

How do I add publications to my profile?
Make sure you are in Edit Profile mode. Scroll to the top of your profile page, and click the **Publications** box in the right column.

LinkedIn adds a Publications section to your profile.

1 Type the name of the book or article in the **Title** field.

2 Type the name of the publisher in the **Publication/Publisher** field.

3 Click the month, day, and year arrows to select the publication month, date, and year in the **Publication Date** field.

4 Type a website address for the publication in the **Publication URL** field.

5 Type the names of any co-authors in the **Authors** field.

6 Type a description of the publication in the **Description** field.

7 Click **Save.**

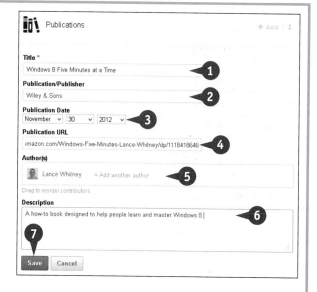

Add Websites to Your Summary, Jobs, and School

I n the section, "Add Websites to Your Profile," you were able to add as many as three website links to your profile. But you can also add specific websites to your summary, to each job, and to your school. For your summary, you can add a blog or other site that promotes your professional accomplishments. For your company or school, you can add a link to its website.

Add Websites to Your Summary, Jobs, and School

1 Make sure you are in Edit Profile mode. Scroll to the top of your profile page, and click the square box arrow (⊡) to the right of the **Edit** link in your summary section.

2 Select **Add Link.**

Note: You can also simply click the link labeled **Add a Link** at the bottom of your summary if that link appears.

3 Type the URL for the website in the **Add a Link** field.

Note: Make sure you type the full name of the site—for example, **www.companyname.com.**

LinkedIn reads and converts the URL into straight text based on the page's description. LinkedIn also displays a logo or image for the website in your summary and fills in the **Description** field.

4 Type a new title and/or description if you do not like the ones created by LinkedIn.

5 Click **Save.**

LinkedIn displays the name and image in your summary.

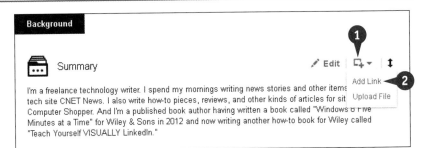

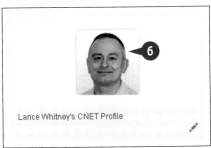

Lance Whitney's CNET Profile

6 Click the website logo or image.

LinkedIn displays a page with the title, image, and description.

7 Click the **Read Original** link to view the actual web page.

LinkedIn displays the page in your browser.

Click the Back button in your browser to return to your LinkedIn profile page.

8 Scroll to the top of the page, and click the **Edit Profile** button if you are no longer in Edit Profile mode.

9 To add a website related to a specific job, move to that job in your profile. Click the square box arrow (⊞) to the right of the **Edit** link, and select **Add Link.**

Repeat steps **4** through **9** to add the link to that job.

10 To add a website related to your school, move to your school in your profile. Click the square box arrow (⊞) to the right of the **Edit** link, and select **Add Link.**

Repeat steps **4** through **9** to add the link to that school.

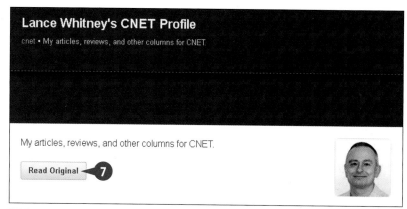

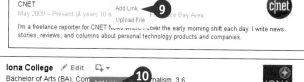

TIP

What types of websites should I add to my profile?
You can certainly add the websites for your company or school. But you will find it more effective to add websites to your own online portfolio or other work in order to highlight your accomplishments.

Upload Files to Your Profile

eyond adding website links, you can upload certain types of files to your profile to highlight your professional achievements. These files include Word documents, PowerPoint presentations, PDFs, and graphic images. You can upload a file to your summary, to each position, and to your education.

Upload Files to Your Profile

1 Make sure you are in Edit Profile mode. Scroll to the top of your profile page, and click the square box arrow (⬚) to the right of the **Edit** link in your summary section.

2 Select **Upload File.**

LinkedIn displays a File Upload window.

3 Double-click the file you want to upload.

LinkedIn uploads and displays the file in your summary and fills in the **Title** and **Description** fields.

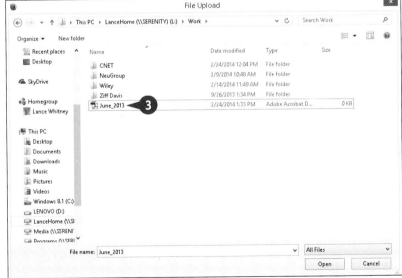

4 Type a new title in the **Title** field and a new description in the **Description** field if you want to change the ones created by LinkedIn.

5 Click **Save.**

LinkedIn displays the name and image in your summary.

6 Click the image of the file to view it.

LinkedIn displays the file.

7 Click the **X** in the upper-right corner of the view page (⊠) to return to your LinkedIn profile page.

8 To upload a file related to a specific job, move to that job in your profile. Click the square box arrow (⊡) to the right of the **Edit** link in your summary section, and **Select Upload File.**

Repeat steps **3** to **7** to add the link to that job.

9 To upload a file related to your school, move to your school in your profile. Click the link labeled **Add a Link,** and repeat steps **3** to **7** to add the link to that school.

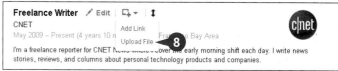

TIP

What is the maximum file size, and what file types can I upload?
The file that you upload may not exceed 100 MB in size and is limited to the following types:

• .pdf	• .pptx	• .potx	• .doc	• .odt	• .jpg
• .ppt	• .ppsx	• .odp	• .docx	• .png	• .jpeg
• .pps	• .pot	• .pdf	• .rtf	• .gif	

Add More Details

Linkedin offers additional categories of information that you can add to your profile. These include honors and awards, test scores, courses, patents, certifications, volunteering and causes, and many more. The steps for adding all these categories and their details are similar to the steps for adding the other categories that are already part of your profile.

Add More Details

1 Make sure you are in Edit Profile mode. Scroll to the top of your profile page.

In the right column, LinkedIn displays a list of other categories, such as **Honors & Awards, Test Scores,** and **Courses.**

2 Click the category that you want to add to your profile.

LinkedIn adds a section for that category to your profile and moves you to that section.

3 Fill in the appropriate fields for that category.

4 Click **Save.**

Repeat those steps for other categories you want to add. After you are finished, scroll to the top of your profile page and click the **Done editing** button.

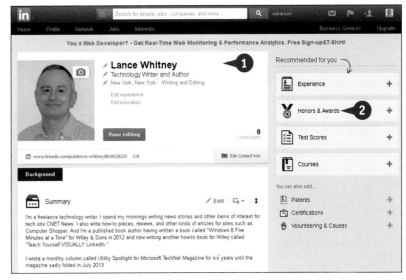

View and Control Your Public Profile

Other LinkedIn members can see your profile. But by default your entire profile is also visible to non-LinkedIn members who may find it through a web search or who know the web address for your profile. You can view your public profile as it appears to non-LinkedIn members and control which details are visible and which ones are not.

View and Control Your Public Profile

1 From any page on LinkedIn, click the **Profile** menu and scroll to the top of your profile page if the page is not already open. Click the link to your public profile. The link starts with www. linkedin.com.

LinkedIn displays your profile as it would appear to the general Internet public.

2 Review your public profile, and then scroll to the bottom of the page and click the **View Full Profile** button.

3 Hover your mouse over the down arrow (▾) next to the **Edit Profile** button, and click **Manage public profile settings.**

LinkedIn again displays your public profile but also shows you a set of options in the right column that let you control the profile.

4 To adjust your public profile so no one outside of LinkedIn can see it, click the **Make my public profile visible to no one** option (○ changes to ◉).

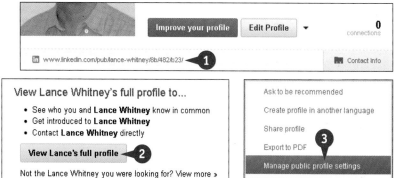

5 If you want to keep your public profile visible but simply hide certain information, leave the option set to **Make my public profile visible to everyone** (◉).

6 Click off any of the listed settings, such as **Picture, Headline, Summary, Current Positions,** and **Past Positions** (☑ changes to ☐).

As you turn off each setting, LinkedIn removes it from your public profile.

7 When you're finished, scroll to the top of the page and click the **View your public profile** link.

LinkedIn opens a new page or tab in your browser and displays your new public page.

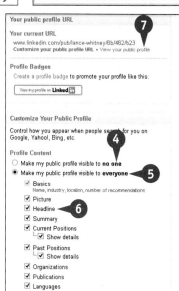

CHAPTER 3

Building Your Network

After you set up your profile, the next step is to build connections with coworkers, employers, employees, classmates, and other fellow LinkedIn members. You can invite people to connect with you as well as accept invitations from others. The idea is to create a mutually beneficial *network* of people with whom you can share job opportunities, career advice, and other items of interest.

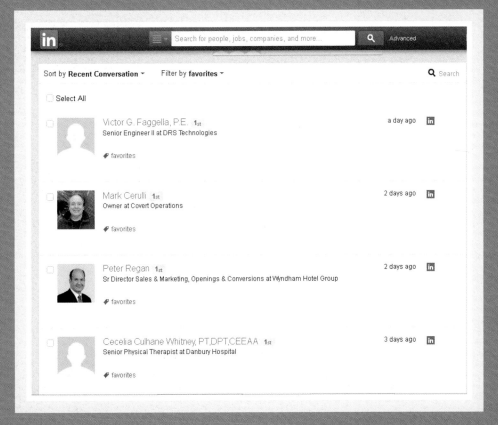

Add Contacts from Your E-Mail

A good spot to look for possible connections is in your own e-mail contact lists. These people likely already know you, at least through e-mail, and so may be ready and willing to connect with you on LinkedIn. You can tap into the address books from a variety of e-mail programs, giving you the ability to invite contacts who are already LinkedIn members as well as those who are not yet members.

Add Contacts from Your E-Mail

1 Log into your LinkedIn account if you do not already have it open. Type your e-mail address and password, and click the **Sign In** button.

2 Click the **Network** menu, and then click **Add Connections.**

3 Select the e-mail service that you want to use.

4 Type your e-mail address in the **Your e-mail** field if it does not already appear, or change it if you do not want to use the displayed address.

5 Click **Continue.**

6 Type your e-mail address and password if prompted, and then click **Sign In** or **Log In.**

LinkedIn may display a window asking for your permission to access your contacts.

7 Click the appropriate button — **Accept, Agree,** or **Yes** — to grant LinkedIn permission to access your contact list.

LinkedIn displays the names of people in your contact list who are already LinkedIn members. By default, all the names in the list are selected (☑).

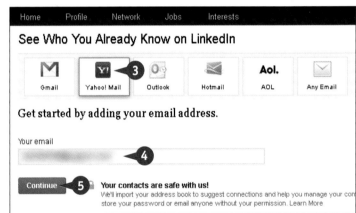

8 Click off the names of any people you do not want to invite to your LinkedIn network (☑ changes to ☐), or click off the **Select all** option and then manually select the names of the people you do want to invite (☐ changes to ☑).

9 Click the **Add Connections** button, or click **Skip this Step** if you do not want to connect with anyone listed.

LinkedIn sends an invitation to the people you selected and then displays the names of people in your contact list who are not LinkedIn members. All names are selected.

10 Click off the names of any people you do not want to invite to your LinkedIn network (☑ changes to ☐), or click off the **Select all** option and then manually select the names of the people you do want to invite (☐ changes to ☑).

11 Click **Add to Network**, or click **Skip this Step** if you do not want to connect with anyone on the list.

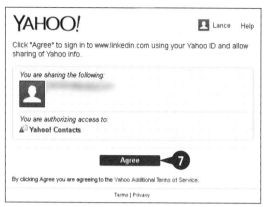

TIPS

What is the difference between a contact and a connection?
Your *contacts* include people with whom you have connected on LinkedIn as well as those you have imported into LinkedIn through an address book. A *connection* is someone with whom you have actually connected on LinkedIn. As such, you may have many contacts who are not necessarily connections.

How does LinkedIn define people who accept your invitations?
Fellow members who accept your invitations are known as *1st-degree connections,* which means you are directly connected with them on LinkedIn.

Accept an Invitation

You can easily make a new connection on LinkedIn by accepting an *invitation* from someone else. The invitation appears as an e-mail in the account that you have set up with LinkedIn. You can automatically accept the invitation from the e-mail or view the person's profile first to decide whether you want to accept.

Accept an Invitation

1. Open the e-mail program or website listed at the primary e-mail account for LinkedIn.

2. View the invitation e-mail from a LinkedIn member with whom you want to connect.

3. Click the **Accept** button to automatically accept the invitation.

   Log into LinkedIn if the site is not already open in your browser.

4. Notice that LinkedIn opens to tell you that you and this person are now connected.

   Alternatively, you may first want to see the profile of a person inviting you to connect before you accept the invitation.

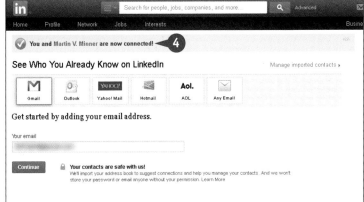

5 To see the profile of the inviter, click the **View Profile** button in the e-mail. Again, log into LinkedIn if the site is not already open.

LinkedIn displays the person's profile page for you to review.

The Invitations flag on your LinkedIn page also displays a number in red (▣), indicating that you have one or more pending invitations.

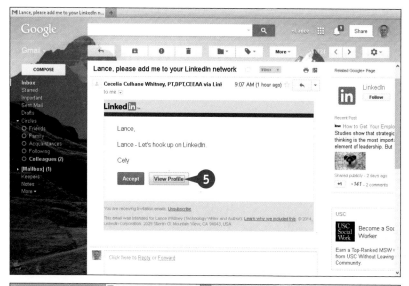

6 Hover your mouse over the red number on the Invitations flag (▣), and then hover over the name of the person.

7 Click the **Ignore** button to disregard the invitation.

8 Click the **Accept** button in the Invitations menu to accept the invitation.

9 Alternatively, click the **Accept Invitation** button at the top of the person's profile.

LinkedIn tells you that you and this person are now connected.

TIP

Should I accept every invitation?
If you know the person by name, you may want to accept the invitation from the e-mail. If not, you should first review the person's profile.

Connect with People You May Know

To help you build your network, LinkedIn steers you to people you may know based on your employers, schools, and current connections. Some of these may be people you do know, while others may indirectly be linked to you by one or two degrees from your existing connections. Either way, you can discover many people who share a common background, job, or profession.

Connect with People You May Know

1 Open your LinkedIn home page if it is not already open.

A small People You May Know section appears in the upper-right column.

Note: The People You May Know section appears only after you have built up your network.

2 Look at the three people shown in that section to see if you want to connect with anyone in this list.

3 Click the **X** (☒) next to the name of anyone with whom you do not want to connect at this point.

4 Hover your mouse over a person's name to see more information.

LinkedIn displays a small window with more details, including the person's current degree of connection to you.

Note: A *2nd-degree connection* means that the person is already linked to one of your 1st-degree connections. A *3rd-degree connection* means that the person is linked to one of your 2nd-degree connections.

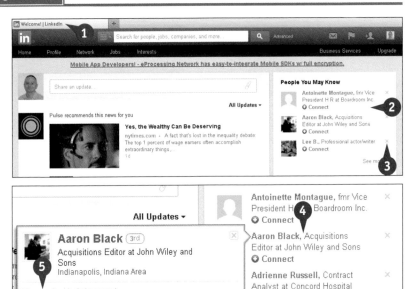

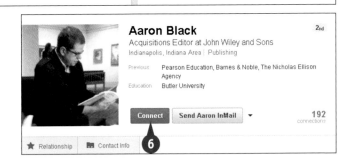

5 Click the **View Profile** link in the details window to see the person's profile.

6 Click the **Connect** button.

7 Click the option that describes how you know this person — **Colleague, Classmate,** or **We've done business together.**

8 Select the company or school through which you know this person.

Note: If you have no current or previous association with the person, but you know this individual personally, you can select the **Friend** option. If you know the person's e-mail address, you can select the **Other** option and then type that e-mail address. Selecting the **I don't know (the person)** option prompts LinkedIn to refuse to send the invitation.

LinkedIn then displays an invitation form.

9 Edit the personal note that this person will receive as part of the invitation.

10 Click the **Send Invitation** button.

LinkedIn displays a message informing you that the invitation has been sent and takes you to the full "People You May Know" page.

TIPS

Why am I not seeing many 2nd- and 3rd-degree connections?
You will not see many 2nd- and 3rd-degree connections until you build up your network.

How do I increase the chances of someone accepting my invitation?
Try to personalize the invitation rather than use the generic invitation text set up by LinkedIn.

How do I personalize the invitation?
Viewing the person's profile and then clicking the **Connect** button gives you the ability to personalize the invitation.

I sent someone an invitation by mistake. Can I cancel it?
Yes, you can withdraw an invitation as follows:

1 Click the **Envelope** icon at the top of any LinkedIn page to open your LinkedIn email.

2 In your Inbox, click the **Sent** folder.

3 Click the subject line of the invitation that you just sent.

4 In the invitation email itself, click the **Withdraw** button.

Search for People

How do you connect with a specific person on LinkedIn? The site offers its own built-in *search* feature through which you can find people to add to your network. You can search for people by name, company, title, location, and other attributes. Searching for connections gives you the ability to find people you know directly as well as those you do not.

Search for People

1 From any LinkedIn page, click the down arrow (■) to the left of the search field at the top of the page.

2 Select **People** from the pop-up menu.

3 Type the first and last names of a person with whom you want to connect, and then click the Search icon (■) or press Enter on your keyboard.

A list of people with that name appears.

Note: If you do not want to search for a person by name, you can search by company, job title, skills, or other criteria.

4 Scroll down the list until you see the person with whom you want to connect.

5 Click the person's name to see the full profile.

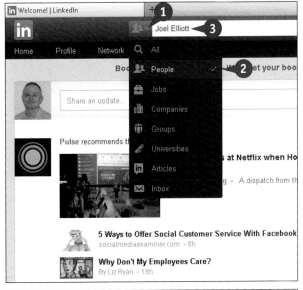

6 Click the **Connect** button to display the form inviting the person to connect on LinkedIn.

7 Edit the personal note, and click the **Send Invitation** button.

LinkedIn displays a message informing you that the invitation has been sent and deposits you at the People You May Know page.

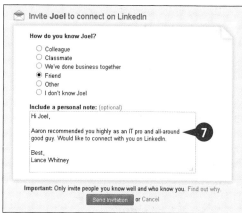

TIP

How can I narrow the search results?

1 To narrow the search results, click one or more of the criteria in the left column. You can filter the results to display people based on relationship, location, current company, industry, past company, school, profile language, and nonprofit interests.

2 Click more criteria. The number of search results decreases.

3 To invite someone to your network, repeat steps 4 through 7.

Find Alumni

Your roommate from college might make a great LinkedIn connection, but you have lost touch over the years. No problem. You can connect with former classmates through the Find Alumni feature. This feature looks at your own schools and others that may interest you and displays the names of any alumni who have LinkedIn accounts.

Find Alumni

1 From any LinkedIn page, click the **Network** menu and then click **Find Alumni.**

LinkedIn displays a page showing fellow students from your college or other school. By default, only those who attended your schools during the same years you did appear.

2 To change the dates, click the arrows (⌄) next to the starting and ending years and click different years.

3 To include all students regardless of year, click the check box to Include people with no dates option (☐ changes to ☑).

By default, LinkedIn shows you alumni who live in your country and in the location you listed in your profile.

4 To narrow the list by a different location, click one or more of the areas listed in the Where they live section.

5 To narrow the list by company, click one or more of the companies in the Where they work section.

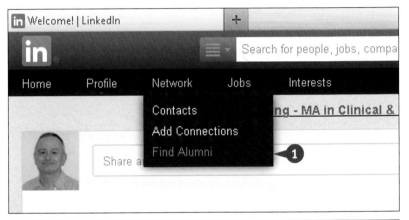

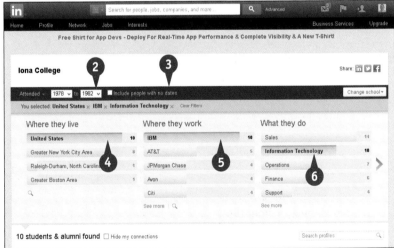

6 To narrow the list by field, click one or more of the fields in the What they do section.

7 To change the selection to a different school, click the **Change school** arrow (⏷).

8 Click the name of another school listed in your profile, or select one of the similar schools suggested by LinkedIn.

9 Alternatively, start typing the name of another school in the **Browse by name** field. Select the school from LinkedIn's list if it appears. Otherwise, continue typing the name of the school.

10 Click the name of a 2nd or 3rd degree alumnus that you want to add to your network.

11 Click the **View Full Profile** button.

12 On the person's profile page, click the **Connect** button or hover over **Send [name of person] InMail** button and click **Connect.**

To send the invitation, repeat steps 6 through 9 from the Connect with People You May Know section in this chapter.

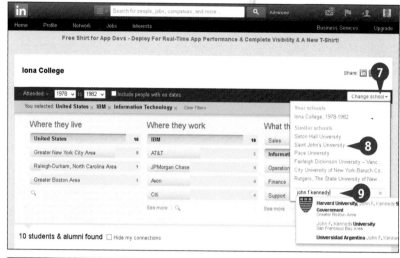

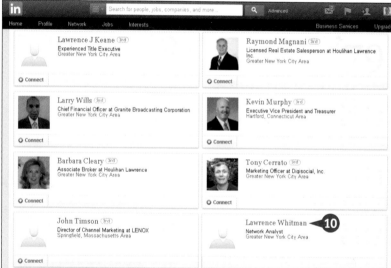

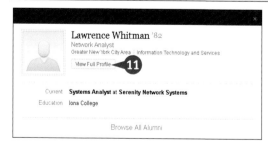

TIP

Why do some items appear in blue?
Blue means the item is selected; clear means the item is not selected.

Get Introduced through a Connection

How can you connect with someone you do not know directly? One of your current connections who knows both of you may be able to help through an *introduction*. This option does rely on the good graces of one of your connections but is a useful option to expand your network beyond those in your inner circles. Only five introductions are available with a free basic account.

Get Introduced through a Connection

1 Find a person you want to invite to your network by following the steps in the "Connect with People You May Know" or "Search for People" sections.

Note: The person with whom you want to connect must be listed as a 2nd- or 3rd-level connection.

2 Click the person's name to view his or her profile.

3 Click the down arrow (⬇) next to the **Send [name of person] InMail** button.

4 Click the **Get introduced** option from the pop-up menu.

LinkedIn suggests one or more shared connections between you and the person.

5 Click the name of the shared connection that you want to use to make the introduction.

LinkedIn displays an invitation form that will be sent to the shared connection.

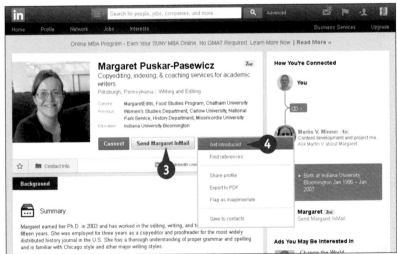

Note: If the person is a 2nd-degree connection, you only need one person to serve the introduction. If the person is a 3rd-degree connection, you have to rely on two go-betweens to ultimately pass along the introduction to its recipient.

⑥ Type a subject in the **Subject** line.

⑦ Type your request in the field to tell the shared connection why you want to get introduced.

⑧ Click the **Send Request** button.

LinkedIn displays a message telling you that your request has been sent.

⑨ Click **Close** to return to the person's profile.

The next step is up to your shared connection to forward the invitation request to the recipient.

Note: You will receive a notice by e-mail informing you if and when the request is approved and the new connection has accepted the invitation.

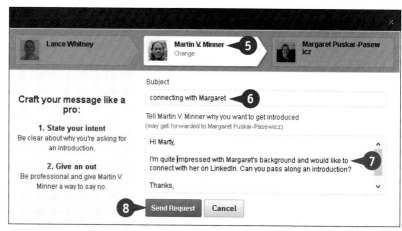

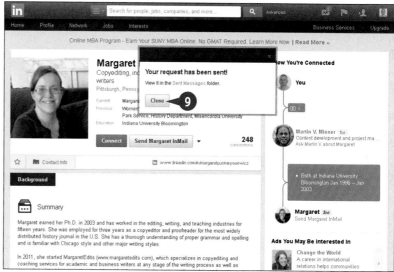

What should I write in the invitation?
Your invitation is directed to your shared connection and may then be seen by the person you want to invite to your network. You should phrase the invitation to tell your shared connection why you want to be introduced.

How can I request more than five introductions?
You need to upgrade to a paid premium account, a process described in Chapter 9. A premium business account offers anywhere from 15 to 35 introductions.

Use InMail

Another way to connect with someone you do not know directly is through an option called *InMail*. This feature allows you to send an invitation to someone without having to rely on a past history or introduction. Sounds great, but there is a catch. LinkedIn members with a free basic account have to pay $10 for each InMail message through LinkedIn's Purchase InMail feature. Those with premium accounts can send a limited number of free messages each month. The process for upgrading to a premium account is described in Chapter 9.

Use InMail

1 To buy a single InMail message, open the Purchase InMail page at https://www. linkedin.com/secure/inmail_ v4. Click the number arrow (⌄) to set the number of InMails you want to purchase.

2 Click **Continue.**

If LinkedIn prompts you to sign in again, type your password.

LinkedIn displays a payment information page that you must complete to pay for the InMail.

3 Complete the payment form, and click the **Review order** button. At the Review your order page, click **Place order.**

Assuming the order goes through, LinkedIn tells you that your order has been processed successfully and displays an online receipt that you can print.

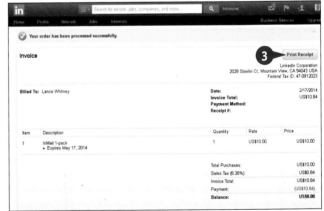

④ Find a person you want to invite to your network via InMail by following the steps in the "Connect with People You May Know" or "Search for People" section.

⑤ Click the name of the person to view his or her profile.

⑥ Click the **Send [name of person] InMail** button.

LinkedIn displays a Compose your message form.

⑦ Keep the check box to **Include my contact information** checked (☑) if you want the person to see your contact info.

⑧ Type your phone number in the **Phone** field if appropriate.

⑨ Click the **Category** down arrow (▾), and select the reason for the InMail.

⑩ Type a subject in the **Subject** field.

⑪ Type a message in the **Your Message** field.

⑫ Click **Send.**

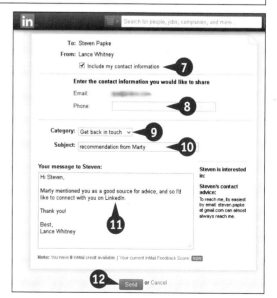

Can I connect with people outside my network?
You can connect with anyone on LinkedIn using InMail, not just 2nd- or 3rd-degree connections.

View the Networks of Your Connections

A nother way to find new connections is to browse the networks of your current ones. Some profiles restrict you from seeing their contacts, but others reveal all their contacts. And because you may know the contacts of your contacts, you might not require an introduction. Otherwise, you can request an introduction though your shared connection.

View the Networks of Your Connections

1 From any LinkedIn page, click the **Networks** menu and then click **Contacts.**

2 Click the name of any contact whose connections you want to see.

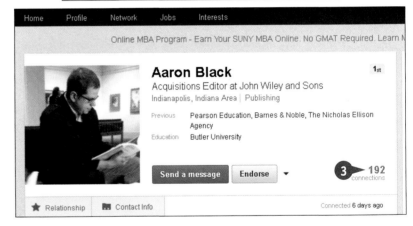

3 At the top of the person's profile, click the blue number above the word "Connections."

Note: If the number is black, then you cannot click it, which means the person's connections are not accessible.

LinkedIn displays a page listing that person's connections.

Note: Some of your connections may restrict the list so you can see only shared connections, meaning people who are already part of your network. In this event, you cannot connect with anyone new.

④ Scroll through each page of connections until you see someone that you want to add to your network.

⑤ Click the person's name and then click the **View profile** button to see that person's profile page.

⑥ To invite a person to your network, click the **Connect** button.

Note: The person who receives your invitation must click the **Send Invitation** button to accept your request.

Repeat steps 6 through 9 from the Connect with People You May Know section to send the invitation.

Alternatively, repeat steps 3 through 7 from the Get Introduced through a Connection section to be introduced through your shared connection.

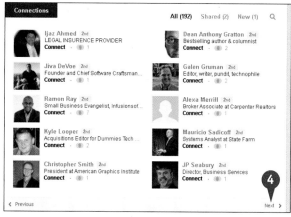

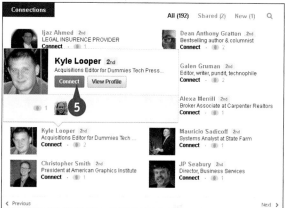

How can I easily see how many people are in my own network?
Open your LinkedIn profile page. The number of connections is listed at the top.

View Your Contacts

After you have built up your network, you need to view and manage all those connections at some point. LinkedIn offers a Contacts page where you can view the people in your network by name, recent conversation, and date you made the connection. You can also filter your contact list by company, title, and other attributes and search for specific people by name.

View Your Contacts

1 From any LinkedIn page, click the **Network** menu and then click **Contacts.**

LinkedIn displays a page showing all your contacts. You can scroll down the page to see all your contacts.

2 Click the name of a contact to see that person's full profile.

3 Click your browser's Back button to return to the contact list.

4 To sort your contact list, click the **Sort by Recent Conversation** arrow (▼) and select one of the other sort options, such as **Last Name, First Name,** or **New.**

5 If you sort by **Last Name** or **First Name,** you can view a specific group of contacts by clicking the **aZ** down arrow (▼) and selecting a specific letter of the alphabet.

6 To filter your contacts by certain criteria, click the **Filter by All Contacts** down arrow (▼) and select one of the specific options, including **Connections Only, Company, Tag, Location, Title,** or **Source.**

7 Depending on the option you choose, you can then select or type a specific name or attribute. For example, if you choose to sort the list by company, you then select or type the name of the company.

8 To revert to all contacts, click the **Filter by** down arrow (▼), click the option you chose to go back one step, and select **All Contacts.**

9 To search for a specific contact, click the Search button (🔍) and start typing the person's name.

LinkedIn displays a list of contacts whose names start with that letter.

10 Select the contact from LinkedIn's list.

TIP

Because the Contacts page shows me LinkedIn connections as well as contacts from my e-mail accounts, how can I identify only the people who are actual LinkedIn connections?
You can identify the members of your LinkedIn network because they have a blue LinkedIn logo next to their profile names.

Tag a Contact

Want to organize your contacts into separate groups? You can do just that by *tagging* them. Using tags, you can categorize and view people based on company, profession, or other criteria. You can also tag a contact as a favorite and view all your favorites together.

Tag a Contact

1 Click the **Network** menu and then click **Contacts** to view a list of your contacts if the Contacts page is not already open.

2 Hover your mouse over the contact you want to tag as a favorite.

3 Click the **Tag** link, and then click the favorites option. Repeat that process for any other contacts you want to tag as favorites.

4 To filter the list of contacts by favorites, scroll to the top of the Contacts page, click the **Filter** arrow (⏷), click the **Tags** option, and select favorites.

Only contacts tagged as favorites appear.

5 Click the **Filter by favorites** arrow (⏷), click **Tag,** and then click **All Contacts** to see all your contacts again.

6 To create a different tag for specific contacts, hover over the name of a contact and click the **Tag** link. Click the option to **Add New Tags.**

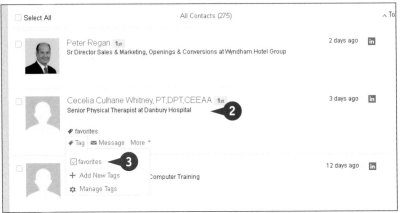

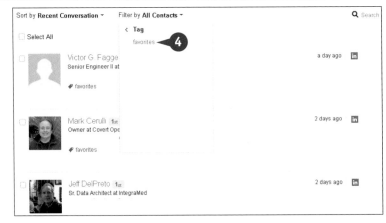

7 Type the name of the new tag, and click **Save.**

8 To add another contact to the new tag group, hover over that contact and click the **Tag** link. Select the new tag, and click anywhere on the page to turn off the Tag menu.

9 To filter the list of contacts by the new tag, scroll to the top of the Contacts page, click the **Filter** arrow (▾), click the **Tags** option, and select the tag you just created.

Only contacts tagged in that new group appear.

10 To manage your tags, hover over any contact, click the **Tags** link, and then click **Manage Tags.**

A list of all tags appears.

11 Click the pencil icon (✎) to change the name of a tag. Type the new name, and click **Save.**

12 Click the **X** (✕) to delete a tag. Click the **Delete** button.

13 Click the **X** (✕) to close the Manage Tags window.

14 Click the **Filter by favorites** arrow (▾), click **Tag,** and then click **All Contacts** to see all your contacts again.

TIP

If I delete a tag, does it delete the actual contact?
No, deleting a tag removes just the tag; it has no effect on the actual contacts.

Hide or Remove a Contact

You can *hide* people from your contact list if you do not want to see them all the time or if you contact list gets too big. You can also remove someone from your network entirely. If you hide a contact, you can always *unhide* that person. But if you remove a connection, you would have to reinvite that person to your network to connect again.

Hide or Remove a Contact

1 Click the **Network** menu and then click **Contacts** to view a list of your contacts if the Contacts page is not already open.

2 Hover over the name of the profile that you want to hide.

3 Click the **More** option, and then click **Hide.** To unhide your hidden connections, scroll to the top of the Contacts page, click the **Filter** arrow, and then click the **Hidden** option.

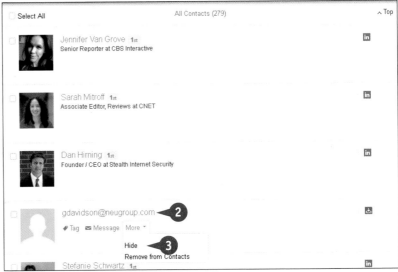

4 Hover over the profile you want to unhide. Click the **More** option, and then click **Unhide.**

5 Scroll to the top of the Contacts page, click the **Filter** arrow (⊡) and click **All Contacts.**

That profile then appears in the All Contacts list.

6 To remove a contact entirely, hover over the profile you want to remove.

7 Click the **More** option, and then click **Remove connection.**

LinkedIn displays a warning telling you what information you would lose if you remove this connection.

8 Click the **Remove** button if you are sure you want to remove the person from your contacts list, or click **Cancel** if you change your mind.

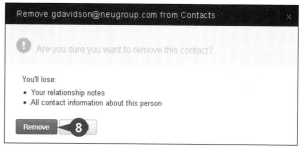

TIP

What happens if I remove a contact or connection?
You can safely remove a contact if you do not think you will ever invite that person to your network. But if you remove a connection, that person will no longer be part of your LinkedIn network unless reinvited.

Select Who Can See Your Connections

By default, your 1st-degree connections can all see each other. But if you want to keep your connections a secret, you can restrict the list so that only you can see that information.

Select Who Can See Your Connections

1 Hover over your small account picture in the upper-right corner to display the **Accounts & Settings** menu.

2 Click the **Review** link for Privacy & Settings.

If required, type your password at the Sign in to LinkedIn page, and click **Sign In.**

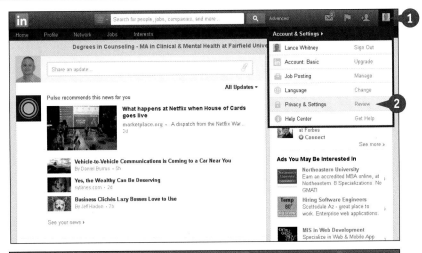

3 At the Privacy & Settings page, click the **Select who can see your connections** link in the Profile section.

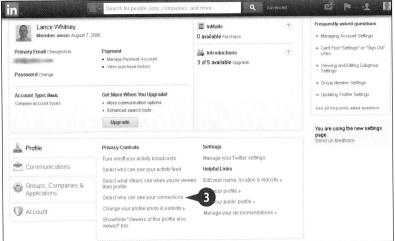

4 In the Who Can See Your Connections window, click the **Your Connections** arrow.

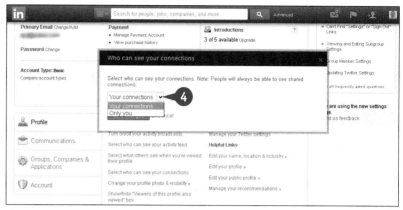

5 Leave the setting to **Your Connections** to allow all your connections to see each other, or change the setting to **Only you** so no one else can see your connections.

6 Click the **Save changes** button.

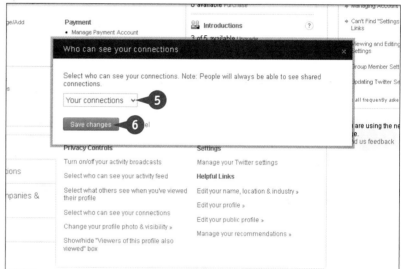

TIPS

How can I easily remove individual contacts imported from one of my e-mail accounts?
As described in the View Your Contacts section, filter your contact list by source and then point the source to the e-mail account in question. You can then scroll down the list and remove any contact who is not a LinkedIn member and whom you do not intend to invite to LinkedIn.

Can I sever the connection between LinkedIn and my e-mail accounts?
Yes. Click the **Settings** icon at the top of the Contacts page. LinkedIn displays a Contacts Settings page. Click the **Remove** button next to the e-mail account that you want to remove from LinkedIn. Note that removing the account does not remove or affect any contacts imported from that account.

CHAPTER 4

Viewing and Posting Updates

After you set up your connections, you can view their posts on your home page. Such posts, or *updates*, can keep you abreast of your connections' professional activities but also offer advice, comments, and information relevant to your career and industry. You can respond to such posts and also post your own updates to share news about you, your company, and other professional interests.

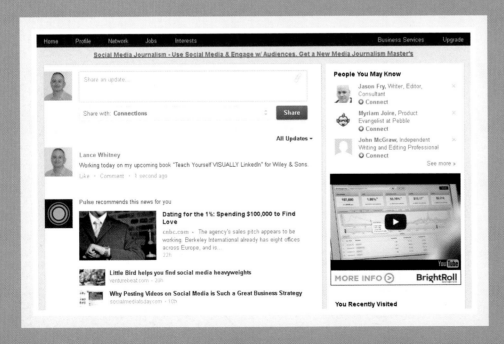

View Updates from Your Connections

Your LinkedIn home page automatically displays the latest updates from the people in your network as well as those from sponsored companies. Many of these updates are worth reading because they can offer news, analysis, and opinions on topics of value to you in your profession.

View Updates from Your Connections

1 From your LinkedIn home page, scroll down to view all the recent updates from people in your network and from sponsored companies.

Some updates include links to articles and other content on web pages.

2 Click the link in an update to view the content.

Click your browser's Back button to return to LinkedIn, or close the tab or page for the web content if LinkedIn opened it separately.

Many updates generate comments from other people. Sometimes, more comments exist than can appear at one time. In that case, LinkedIn displays a **Show previous comments** link.

3 Find an update with the **Show previous comments** link, and click that link to view past comments.

Page numbers may appear under the **Add a comment** field.

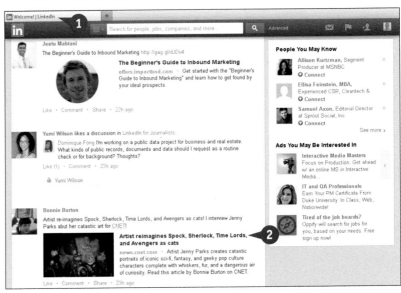

④ Click the page number 1 to see the first several comments to the update. You can then click each successive page number to view all the comments.

Click your browser's Back button to return to the full LinkedIn page.

⑤ Scroll to the top of your page, and hover over the **All Updates** link.

⑥ Click **Top** to see the top updates first.

⑦ Hover over the **All Updates** link again, and click **Recent** to see the most recent updates first.

⑧ Hover over the **All Updates** link again.

⑨ Click each option in the **All Updates** menu to filter the updates you see to only those shared, only those from connections, only updates about someone's profile, and more.

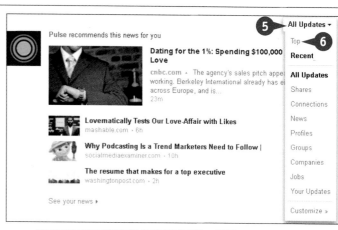

⑩ Hover over the **All Updates** link again, and click **All Updates** to remove the filter.

⑪ To hide an update and all future updates from a certain account, hover over one of that account's updates and click the **Hide** link.

⑫ To unhide that person's updates, click the **Undo** link on the update notice.

TIP

What is a sponsored update?
A sponsored update is a way for a business or other organization to post an update about itself that it hopes will interest LinkedIn members.

Manage which Updates You See

Inundated by too many updates on your home page? You can manage which updates you see by controlling them from LinkedIn's "Updates you see on your home page" window. Here, you can hide any type of update and unhide it if you want to see it again. You can also set how many updates appear on your home page at one time.

Manage which Updates You See

1 From your LinkedIn home page, hover over the **All Updates** link and click **Customize.**

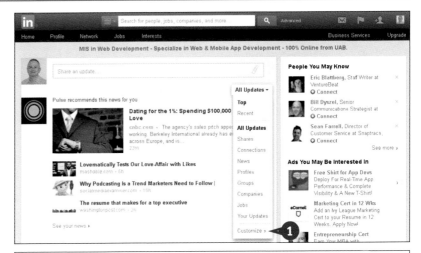

2 If LinkedIn prompts you to sign in again, type your password and click the **Sign In** button.

LinkedIn displays an "Updates you see on your home page" window.

3 Click to turn off any updates you do not want to see (☑ changes to ☐).

4 If you have hidden any updates and want to unhide them, click the **Hidden** tab and click the updates you want to see (☑ changes to ☐).

5 Click the arrow under **How many updates do you want on your homepage?**(☑), and change the number of updates.

6 Click the **Save Changes** button.

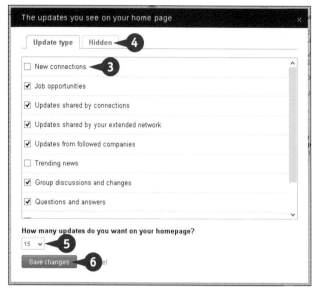

7 Click the **Home** menu to return to your LinkedIn home page.

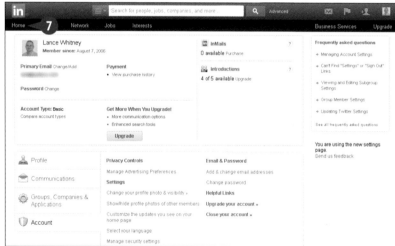

Should I limit the number of updates I receive?

Not necessarily. You may want to allow all updates initially and then pare them down one by one if you find yourself inundated by too many.

Respond to an Update

Want to add your own two cents to a particular update? You can *respond* to an update by commenting on it, as well as by liking it and sharing it with the people in your network. Your comment may then elicit a response from the person who posted the update and from other people who read it, triggering a lengthier conversation thread.

Respond to an Update

1 From the LinkedIn home page, scroll down to view all the recent updates from people in your network and from sponsored companies.

2 Choose an update to which you want to add a comment.

3 Type your comment in the comment field.

4 Click the **Comment** button.

Your comment appears below the update.

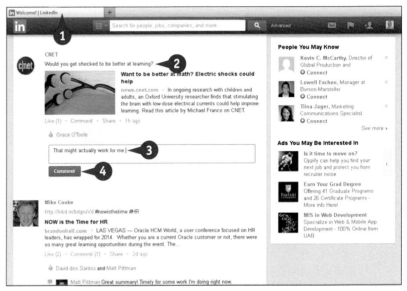

5 To like an update, click the **Like** link.

The Like number goes up by one to indicate that your Like went through. You are also listed as one of the people who likes the update.

6 To share an update, click the Share link.

LinkedIn displays a Share window.

7 Type something in the text box of the Share window if you want to comment on the update.

8 Click the **Share with: Public** arrow (⬚), and select **Connections** if you want to share the update only with the people in your immediate network.

9 Click the **Twitter** check box (☐ changes to ☑) if you want to share the update with your Twitter followers.

10 Click the **Send to Individuals** check box (☐ changes to ☑) if you want to share the update with certain people via e-mail.

11 Type the name or e-mail address of the person with whom you want to share the update, and then type a personal message if needed.

Note: You can choose to share an update both on LinkedIn and through e-mail, or just stick with one of those options.

12 Click the **Share** button to share the update.

LinkedIn displays a notification telling you that you have successfully shared the update.

13 Click **Close** to close the notification message.

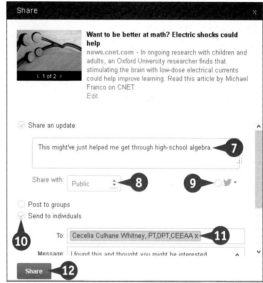

TIP

Who can see my updates?
Any update you share with the public is viewable by your 1st-degree connections as well as your 2nd- and 3rd-degree connections.

Post Your Own Updates

You can share information about yourself and your job or career by posting an update with the latest news. But you can also share general items that you think would interest the people in your network. You can post your own updates to share key information with your entire network, which includes your 2nd- and 3rd-degree connections, or only with your direct 1st-degree connections.

Post Your Own Updates

Share a Text Update

1 Scroll to the top of your LinkedIn home page. In the **Share an Update** field, type your update.

2 Click the **Share with public** arrow (⊡), and choose whether to share this update with the public, only with your connections, or with your connections and Twitter followers.

Note: The option to share with your Twitter followers appears only if you have set up your Twitter account in LinkedIn.

3 Click the **Share** button.

Your update appears.

Attach a File to an Update

1 To attach a file to a new update, click the paper clip icon (🖉) in the upper-right corner of the Update window.

LinkedIn displays a File Upload window.

2 Browse to and double-click the file that you want to upload from your PC.

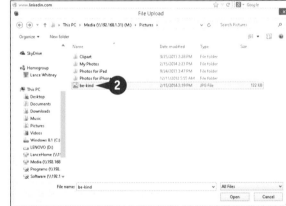

82

LinkedIn uploads and converts your file. The file appears as a thumbnail as part of your update.

Type your update in the update field, shown in Step 1 of "Share a Text Update."

Click the **Share with public** arrow (⬚), shown in Step 2 of "Share a Text Update." Choose whether to share this update with the public, only with your connections, or with your connections and Twitter followers.

Click **Share,** shown in Step 3 of "Share a Text Update."

Your update appears.

Share a Website Link

1 To share a website link, open a new tab or page in your browser and navigate to the web page you want to share.

2 Select the site's address in the **URL** field.

3 Right-click the selected address, and click **Copy** from the pop-up menu.

4 Return to your LinkedIn page.

5 Right-click in the **Update** field, and click **Paste** from the pop-up menu.

LinkedIn displays a link, thumbnail, and description for the website in the **Update** field.

Delete the web address from the **Update** field, shown in Step 1 of "Share a Text Update," and type your update message.

Click the **Share with public** arrow (⬚), shown in Step 2 of "Share a Text Update." Choose whether to share this update with the public, only with your connections, or with your connections and Twitter followers.

Click **Share,** shown in Step 3 of "Share a Text Update."

Your update appears.

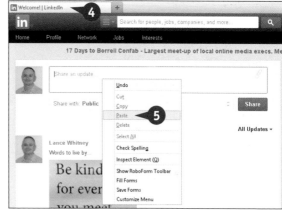

TIP

What information should I share in an update?
You can share information about your latest professional accomplishments but also try to share general information and advice that you think would interest your connections.

Link to a Name in an Update

Mention the name of a person or company on LinkedIn in an update, and you can create a link directly to that name. Linking to a name this way makes it easier for those who read your updates to find more information about the people and companies you mention.

Link to a Name in an Update

1 Scroll to the top of your LinkedIn home page. Click in the **Share an Update** field.

2 Start typing your update. Press the @ key, and LinkedIn shows you some of the connections and companies that start with the letter A.

3 Type the first letter of the connection or company to which you want to refer after the @. LinkedIn shows you some connections and companies that start with that letter.

4 Continue typing the name until you see it on the list. From the list, click the name of the connection or company that you want to refer to in your update.

5 Finish typing your update.

6 Click the **Share with public** arrow (⬍), and choose whether to share this update with the public, only with your connections, or with your connections and Twitter followers.

7 Click the **Share** button.

Your update appears with the connection or company linked and underlined in blue.

8 Hover over the link for the connection if you included one in your update.

LinkedIn displays a window with options to send a message or view the profile of your connection.

9 Hover over the link for a company if you included one in your update.

LinkedIn displays a window with a description of the company and links to follow it and see its jobs and careers.

TIP

How many links can I include in a single update?
You can include as many links as you want, which can be useful if you need to list the names of several people or companies in a single update.

Delete One of Your Updates

Oops, you made a mistake with one of your updates and want to *delete* it. No problem. You can remove an update so that it is no longer visible to your connections. Keep in mind, however, that people may have already read it. But better late than never.

Delete One of Your Updates

1 Hover over the **All Updates** link on your LinkedIn Page.

2 Click the option to show **Your Updates.**

Only your updates are visible.

3 Hover over the update you want to remove.

4 Click **Delete.**

LinkedIn displays a message asking if you are sure you want to delete this update.

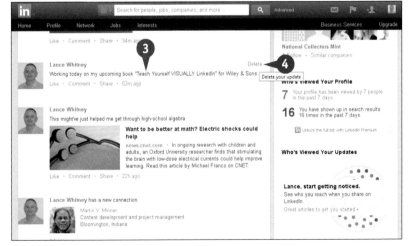

5 Click the **Cancel** button if you choose not to; otherwise, click the **Delete** button to remove it.

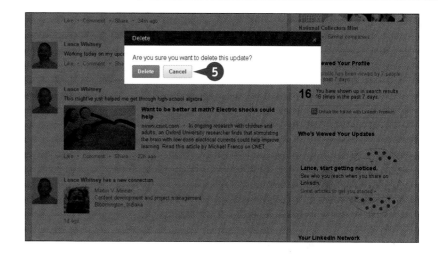

Why would I delete an update?

You might delete an update if it contains a typo or other mistake. You might also delete it if, in retrospect, you feel the update is not appropriate or relevant to other LinkedIn members.

What happens with an update that I delete?

It depends on the type of update and how quickly you delete it after you post it. According to LinkedIn, deleting an update removes it from the updates section on the home pages of your connections. But if some time has passed before you delete an update, it could still appear in a digest e-mail sent to your connections.

Are there any updates that I cannot delete?

An update that shows you have made a new connection cannot be deleted. But these types of updates are posted automatically by LinkedIn.

See Who's Viewed Your Recent Updates

ant to see how many people are actually reading your updates? LinkedIn can share that information with you. You can see how many people have viewed, liked, and commented on one of your updates. LinkedIn even shows you the number of views among your 1st-, 2nd-, and 3rd-degree connections.

See Who's Viewed Your Recent Updates

1 Scroll down your LinkedIn home page until you see a section in the right column called "Who's Viewed Your Updates."

LinkedIn sequentially displays your last several updates with information on how many views, likes, and/or comments each one has received.

2 Hover over the first few words of a specific update to view the full update.

The inner circle in the section tells you how many of your 1st-degree connections viewed, liked, and commented on a particular update.

3 Hover over the inner circle.

LinkedIn displays a message showing how many of your 1st-degree connections responded to the update.

4 Move your mouse to the next circle.

LinkedIn displays a message showing how many 2nd-degree connections, if any, responded to the update.

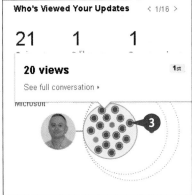

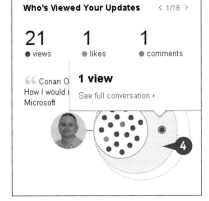

5 Hover your mouse over the outer circle.

LinkedIn displays a message showing how many 3rd-degree connections, if any, responded to the update.

6 Click the right arrow (▷) to the right of Who's Viewed Your Updates to move to the next update.

7 Repeat steps 3 through 6 to see the number of views, likes, and comments for this update and additional updates.

An update that has received comments or likes represents the total number of responses with a series of dots.

8 Hover over the orange dot representing a comment to read that comment.

9 Hover over the green dot representing a like to read that like.

10 Return to the first update and click the left arrow (◁) to move back one step.

11 Review the updated results. LinkedIn shows you the total number of views, likes, and comments for all your latest updates.

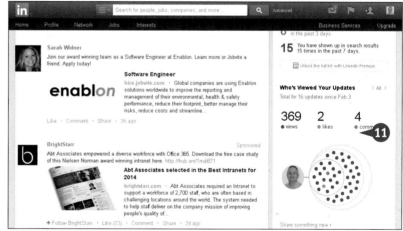

How can I increase the viewership of my updates?
Use an appealing headline and try to comment on your own update to generate interest and trigger a potential conversation.

CHAPTER 5

Communicating with Other People

After you set up your network, you can then stay in touch with your connections through e-mail. You can e-mail any of your 1st-degree connections, and they in turn can e-mail you. LinkedIn also keeps track of your incoming and outgoing messages so you can easily view and manage them.

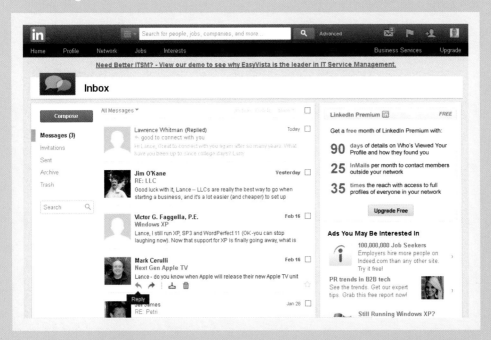

E-Mail a Connection

Need to contact one of your connections about something private? LinkedIn has its own e-mail feature. You can view a list of all your connections through LinkedIn's Contacts page. From there, you can easily select the person you want to e-mail and then compose and send your message.

E-Mail a Connection

1 From any LinkedIn page, hover over the **Network** menu and click **Contacts.**

2 Scroll down the list of Contacts until you find the person you want to e-mail.

3 Hover over that person's listing, and click the **Message** link.

LinkedIn displays a message window.

4 Type the subject of the message in the **Subject** field.

5 Type the body of the message in the **Add Your Message** field.

6 Click the **Send Message** button.

LinkedIn flashes a notice telling you that your message was sent and returns you to the Contacts page.

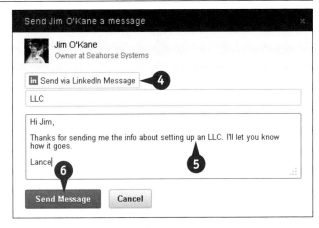

TIP

Can I e-mail someone without having to open the Contacts page?
Yes, you can e-mail someone directly from your LinkedIn e-mail inbox. Simply click the envelope icon in the upper bar at the top of any LinkedIn page. From your inbox, click the **Compose** button at the top of the page. Then address, compose, and send your e-mail.

Check for New E-Mails

Any e-mail sent to you on LinkedIn is automatically passed along through the primary e-mail account that you registered with the site. So you will find new messages from your LinkedIn connections in your regular e-mail. But you can also check for new e-mail right from LinkedIn as well.

Check for New E-Mails

1 Open the e-mail account registered with LinkedIn, and open an e-mail from one of your LinkedIn connections.

E-mails from a LinkedIn connection display the name, potentially a photo of the sender, and the message itself.

2 Open your LinkedIn home page.

New messages are indicated by a red box with a number ( ) on the envelope icon in the upper bar. The number indicates the number of new and unread messages.

3 Hover over the envelope icon.

The last three of your unread e-mails appear in the list.

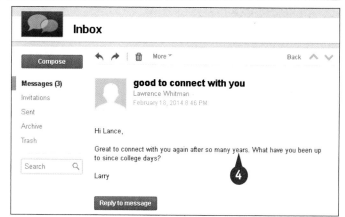

4 Click the sender's name to view the full message in your LinkedIn inbox.

LinkedIn opens your e-mail inbox to display the entire message.

Respond to an E-Mail

You can respond to a new e-mail in one of three ways — through your own e-mail account, through the e-mail notification icon on the top bar of your LinkedIn home page, or from your LinkedIn e-mail inbox. You can also respond to an older e-mail by opening your inbox directly.

Respond to an E-Mail

1 Open the e-mail account registered with LinkedIn.

2 Open the LinkedIn e-mail to which you want to respond.

3 Click the **Reply to [name of sender]** button.

Your LinkedIn inbox opens. The blinking cursor points to the location where you can type your response.

4 Type your response.

5 Click the **Send Message** button.

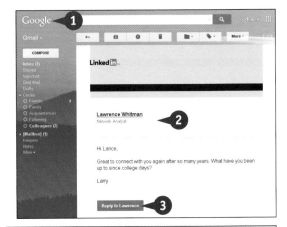

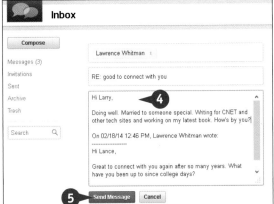

6 Alternatively, open your LinkedIn home page.

New messages are indicated by the red box with a number ( ) on the envelope icon in the upper bar.

7 Hover over the envelope icon.

Your newest e-mails appear in the list.

8 Click **Reply** to open your inbox.

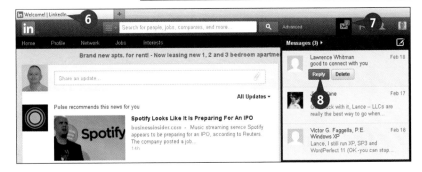

9 You can now read the full message, reply to it, and send your response.

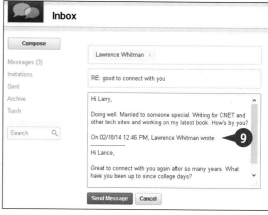

10 To respond to an older e-mail, scroll through your inbox until you find the e-mail to which you want to respond.

11 Click the reply arrow (↩).

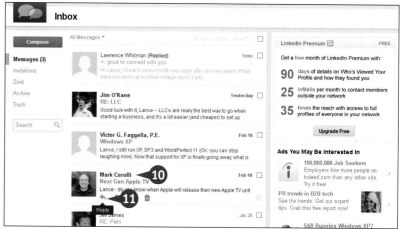

12 Repeat steps **3** through **5** to respond to the sender.

Where can I see my reply after I send it?
Your reply appears as a message in your Sent folder with the text from the original e-mail included as well.

What do you do with a new LinkedIn e-mail that you have already read or do not need to read? You can easily delete it from any page. You can also delete, archive, and forward older e-mails from your LinkedIn inbox.

Manage Individual E-Mails

Delete an E-mail

1 To delete a new e-mail, hover over the envelope icon in the bar at the top of the page.

2 Click **Delete** for the e-mail you want to delete.

LinkedIn deletes the message.

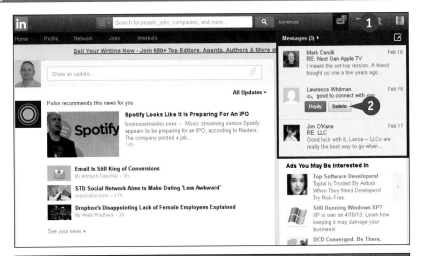

3 To delete an older e-mail, click the envelope icon on the top bar (shown in step **1**) to open your inbox if it is not already open.

Then hover over the e-mail you want to delete, and click **Delete**.

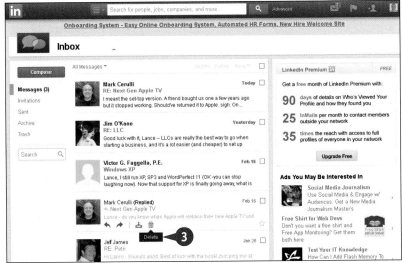

Forward an E-mail

1 To forward an e-mail to another person, hover over the e-mail you want to forward.

2 Click **Forward** (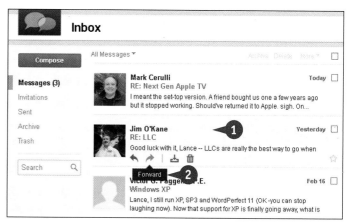).

LinkedIn displays a form that you can fill out to forward the message.

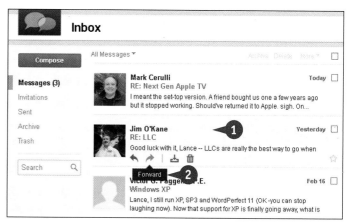

3 Click in the **To** field and start typing the name of the LinkedIn connection to whom you want to forward the message.

LinkedIn displays a list of names matching the first few characters you type.

4 Select the name of the contact from LinkedIn's list.

5 Change the subject if needed.

6 Type a message at the top of the message field above the forwarded text.

7 Click the **Send Message** button.

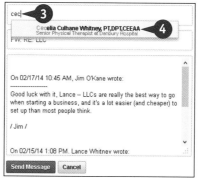
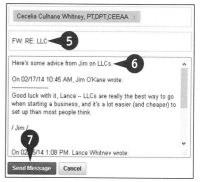

Archive an E-mail

1 To archive an e-mail, hover over the e-mail you want to archive.

2 Click the **Archive** button.

LinkedIn moves the message from your inbox to the Archive folder.

TIP

How can I see my archived messages?
You can see all archived messages by clicking the Archive folder in the left column.

View and Manage All Your LinkedIn E-Mail

Beyond managing individual e-mails, you can view and manage the e-mail folders in your inbox. You can then easily delete or archive messages that you no longer need. LinkedIn uses five different folders to store different types of messages: Messages, Invitations, Sent, Archive, and Trash.

View and Manage All Your LinkedIn E-Mail

1 From any LinkedIn page, click the envelope icon in the bar at the top of the page if you are not already at your Inbox page.

LinkedIn opens your inbox.

2 To see all the messages you have received, scroll through the **Messages** folder.

Note: Clicking the right arrow at the bottom (▶) moves you forward one page, the left arrow (◀) moves you back one page, the right arrow with the vertical bar (▶|) moves you to the last page, and the left arrow with the vertical bar (◀|) moves you to the first page.

3 To see any pending invitations from other LinkedIn members, click and scroll through the **Invitations** folder.

4 To see all your sent messages, click and browse through the **Sent** folder.

5 To see all your archived messages, click and browse through the **Archive** folder.

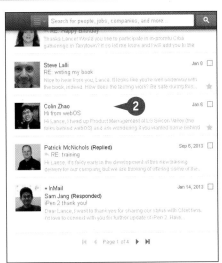

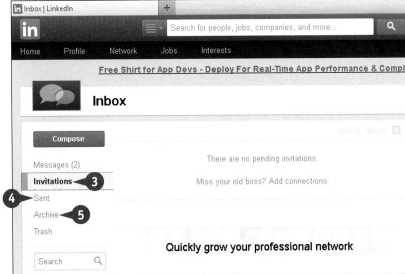

6 To see all your deleted messages, click and browse through the **Trash** folder.

7 Select your Archive folder.

8 Scroll to the bottom of the page, and click the right arrow with the vertical bar (⏭) to move to the last page.

9 Click the check box at the upper-right next to the **Delete** and **More** options (☐ changes to ☑).

All the messages on your current page are checked.

10 Click the **Delete** option to delete all the messages on your current page.

Note: Only the messages on your current page are removed; all other messages in that folder remain.

11 Click the **Trash** folder.

12 Select one or more messages that you want to undelete by clicking their check boxes in the upper right (☐ changes to ☑).

13 Click the **Undelete** option.

The messages are undeleted and sent to your Messages folder.

Note: Older messages may be sent to your Archive folder.

TIP

How do I select all the messages on my current page?
You can check the check box in the upper-right corner (☐ changes to ☑) to select all the messages on your current page.

99

Search Your Inbox for Specific Messages

You need to find a specific e-mail but are having trouble tracking it down. No problem. You can search for specific messages within your entire inbox based on names, titles, companies, and other keywords. LinkedIn retrieves any messages that contain the word you specified. You can also fine-tune a search by typing multiple words or an entire phrase.

Search Your Inbox for Specific Messages

1 From any LinkedIn page, click the envelope icon at the top of the page if your Inbox is not already open.

LinkedIn opens your inbox.

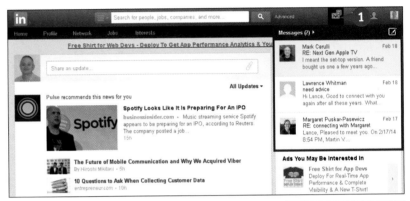

2 Type a word in the Search box.

Note: You can type a person's name or another word that you know appears in at least one of your e-mails.

3 Click the search icon (🔍) or Press **Enter** on your keyboard.

LinkedIn displays a list of all e-mails across all folders that contain the word you typed. LinkedIn also points to the e-mail's folder.

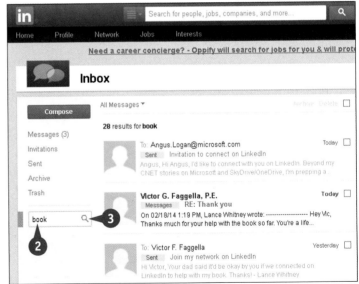

④ Type a series of words or a phrase in the **Search** field, and click the search icon (🔍).

LinkedIn displays a list of e-mails that contain any of the words you typed.

⑤ Type two words in the search field with the word **AND** in uppercase between them, and click the search icon (🔍).

LinkedIn responds with a list of e-mails that contain both of those words.

⑥ Type a phrase enclosed in quotes, and click the search icon (🔍).

LinkedIn responds with a list of e-mails that contain that specific phrase.

⑦ Type two words with a hyphen in front of the second word, for example, linkedin –invitation, and click the search icon (🔍).

LinkedIn responds with a list of e-mails that contain the first word but not the second word.

Set the Frequency of E-Mails

orried about getting swamped by e-mails from LinkedIn? You can control how frequently you receive LinkedIn e-mails for messages from other members, updates, and other content. You can also set whether you want to receive each individual e-mail, an e-mail digest, or no e-mail at all.

Set the Frequency of E-Mails

1 Click the small account picture in the upper-right corner to display the **Accounts & Settings** menu.

2 From the **Accounts & Settings** menu, click the **Review** link for Privacy & Settings.

If required, type your password at the Sign in to LinkedIn page.

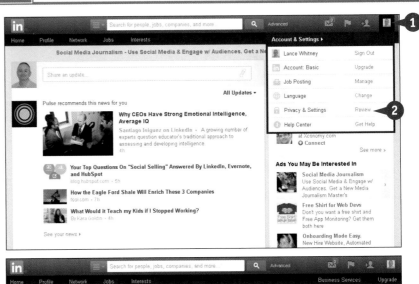

3 At the Privacy & Settings page, click the tab for **Communications** and then click the link for **Set the frequency of e-mails.**

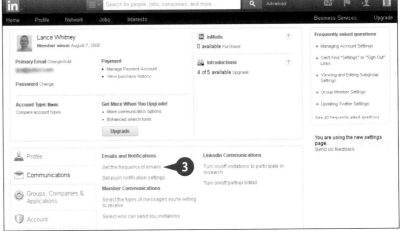

④ At the E-mail frequency page, click the first setting: **Messages from other members.**

⑤ Click the **Invitations to connect** arrow (⌄), and select whether you want to receive an individual e-mail for each invitation, a weekly e-mail digest listing all invitations for that week, or no e-mail at all.

⑥ Click each of the other categories in the Messages from other members section, and select one of the available options if you want to change the current option.

⑦ Click the **Save Changes** button when you're finished.

⑧ Click the second setting: **Updates and news.**

⑨ Click the **Network updates** arrow (⌄), and select **Daily Digest E-mail, Weekly Digest E-mail,** or **no E-mail.**

⑩ Click the **Save Changes** button.

⑪ Click the fourth setting: **Notifications.**

⑫ Click the **Notifications** summary arrow (⌄), and select one of the available options.

⑬ Click each of the other categories in the Notifications summary section, and select one of the available options if you want to change the current option.

⑭ Click the **Save Changes** button.

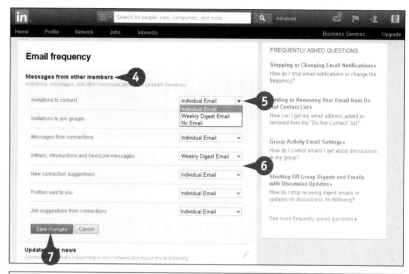

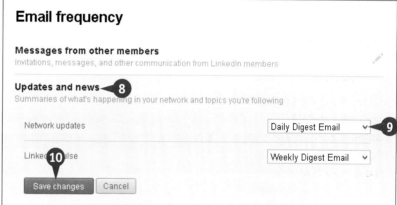

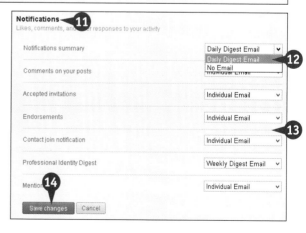

Select Who Can Send You Invitations

You can change your settings to determine who can send you invitations, such as only people on LinkedIn, only people who know your e-mail address and appear in your "Imported Contacts" list, or only those who appear in your "Imported Contacts" list.

Select Who Can Send You Invitations

1 Click your small account picture in the upper-right corner to display the Accounts & Settings menu.

2 From the **Accounts & Settings** menu, click the **Review** link for Privacy & Settings.

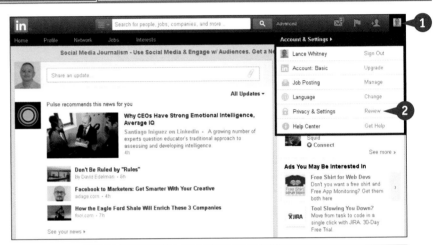

3 If required, type your password at the Sign in to LinkedIn page.

4 At the Privacy & Settings page, click the tab for **Communications** and then click the link for **Select who can send you invitations.**

5 At the Who can send you invitations window, click the button (◉ changes to ◉) to set who can send you invitations: **Anyone on LinkedIn (Recommended); Only people who know your e-mail address or appear in your "Imported Contacts" list; or Only people who appear in your "Imported Contacts" list.**

6 Click the **Save Changes** button.

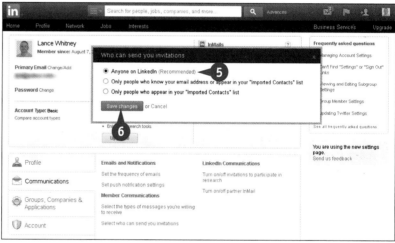

Why does LinkedIn recommend that I use the setting for Anyone on LinkedIn?

Using the setting for **Anyone on LinkedIn** ensures that you can receive invitations from every LinkedIn member, not just people you know.

What does LinkedIn mean by my "Imported Contacts" list?

As described in the "Add Contacts from Your E-mail" task in Chapter 3, you can import into LinkedIn the names and e-mail addresses of your contacts from Gmail, Yahoo! Mail, or other e-mail accounts. You can

then opt to invite any of your contacts to your LinkedIn network or accept invitations from any of them.

What would happen if I restrict invitations to only people who know my e-mail address or appear in my "Imported Contacts" list?

You would receive invitations only from people you know or who know you, restricting your ability to grow your network. Remember that you can choose to receive invitations from anyone on LinkedIn and then simply ignore any individual invitations that you do not want to accept.

CHAPTER 6

Revising Your Profile

At some point after you have set up your basic profile page, you likely will want to go back to enhance or revise certain details. You may want to rewrite or add certain information to spruce up your profile. Or you may simply need to update various items, such as your current job, your location, or your contact info as that information changes.

 Experience   **+ Add a position** | ↕

Freelance Writer Edit | ▾ | ↕

CNET News

May 2009 – Present (4 years 10 months)

I'm a freelance reporter for CNET News where I cover the early morning shift each day. I write news stories, reviews, and columns about personal technology products and companies.

Each day brings new surprises, so the work is interesting and challenging and keeps me on my toes.

Lance Whitney's CNET Profile

Change Your Name, Headline, or Location

If your name changes, you can easily change it in your profile as well. You may also want to revise your headline if you think of something snappier. And you can change your location if you move, and your industry if you switch careers.

Change Your Name, Headline, or Location

1 From any LinkedIn page, hover over the **Profile** menu and click **Edit Profile.**

2 To change your name, click the pencil icon ( ) in front of your name.

3 Enter your new first and/or last name.

4 To enter your former name, click the **Former Name** link and type the former name you want to display. Click the **Save** button.

Note: In this section, you can also choose whether your name is visible to all your connections, your entire network, or everyone who sees your profile.

Note: My Connections refers to your 1st-degree connections. **My Network** refers to 1st-, 2nd-, and 3rd-degree connections. **Everyone** refers to all LinkedIn users who can see your profile.

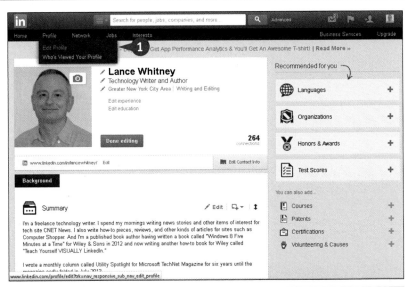

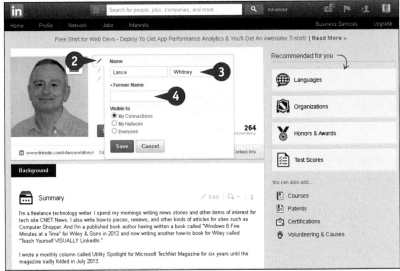

5 To change your professional headline, click the pencil icon (✐) in front of your current title.

6 Click the **Show examples** link to get some ideas for a headline.

7 Click the link to **See what others in your industry are using** to view the titles used by colleagues in your line of work.

8 Type your new title in the field under **Your professional headline.** Click **Save.**

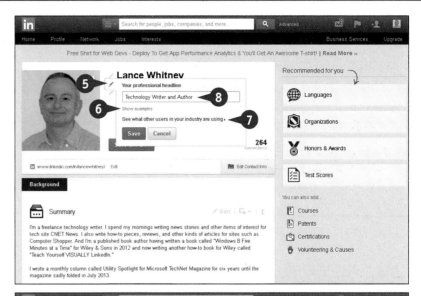

9 To change your location, click the pencil icon (✐) in front of the current location.

10 If necessary, change the country at the top.

11 Type your new ZIP Code in the **Postal code** field.

12 A list of location names that you used in the past may also appear below the postal code. If one of these names matches your current location, select it.

13 To change your industry, click the current selection under the **Industry** title and select your new industry.

14 Click **Save.**

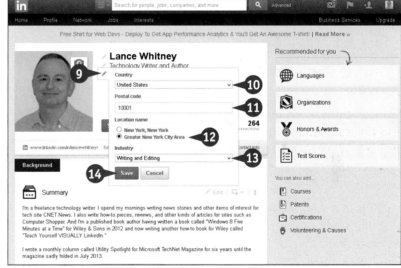

TIP

How can I create a good headline?
Stumped coming up with your own headline? Be sure to look at examples of headlines and see what others in your industry are using.

Change Your Photo

You can adjust your current photo by resizing it and changing its position, or you can remove it entirely and replace it with a different photo. You can also preview your photo as you tweak it to see how it will look when it appears in your profile.

Change Your Photo

1 To change your photo in Profile edit mode, click the camera icon (⬚) in the upper-right corner of your current image.

LinkedIn displays the Edit Photo window.

2 If you want to keep your current photo but simply resize it, click and drag the yellow block in the lower-right corner of the larger yellow square. Drag the block diagonally to resize the image.

3 When you're finished resizing the image, move your cursor to the center of the large square. Move your cursor to crop the image.

LinkedIn's Preview window shows you how the image will appear.

4 Click **Save**.

Your revised photo appears in your profile.

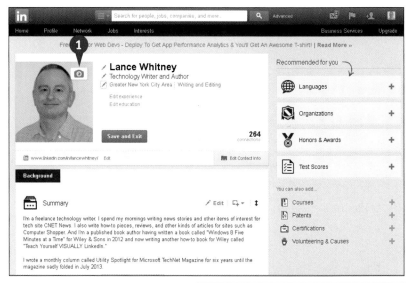

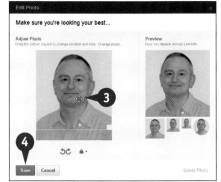

5 To replace your photo with a new one, again click the photo icon (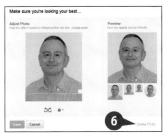), that appears in the upper-right corner of your current image.

LinkedIn displays the Edit Photo window.

6 Click the **Delete Photo** link.

LinkedIn removes your picture and brings you back to your Profile page.

7 Click the **Add a Photo** link.

LinkedIn displays the Edit Photo window.

8 In the Edit Photo window, click the **Browse** button.

LinkedIn displays the File Upload window.

9 Browse to and double-click the file you want to upload.

10 Resize and position the photo accordingly. Click **Save**.

Your new photo appears in your profile.

TIP

Does LinkedIn have to approve my photo?
No, but LinkedIn may remove your photo if the image is not your likeness or is not a headshot photo.

Add or Update an E-Mail Address

You can add another e-mail address to your contact info if you have more than one e-mail account. For example, you may want to list both your personal and work addresses, especially if you use both for professional reasons. You can also add a new e-mail address and remove the old one if your address has changed.

Add or Update an E-Mail Address

1 To add another e-mail address in Profile Edit mode, click the **Edit Contact Info** link.

2 In the Contact Info section, click the pencil icon (✐) next to your e-mail address.

If LinkedIn prompts you to sign in, type your password and click the **Sign In** button.

LinkedIn displays an Add & change e-mail addresses window.

3 Type your new e-mail address in the e-mail address field. Click the **Add email address** button.

LinkedIn sends a confirmation e-mail to the address you entered.

4 Click the **Go to your mail** button to open the confirmation e-mail.

Your e-mail account opens.

5 Open the LinkedIn E-mail Confirmation message, and click the link in the message to confirm your address.

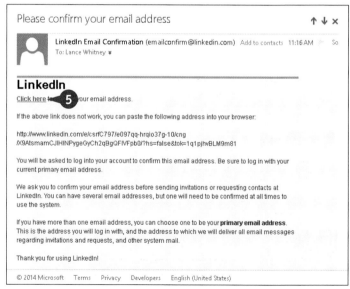

LinkedIn confirms your address and returns you to your home page.

Note: You can close your e-mail if it is still open in a separate web page or tab.

6 Hover over the **Profile** menu, and click **Edit Profile.** Click the **Edit Contact Info** link, and then click the pencil icon (✏) for your e-mail address.

If LinkedIn prompts you to sign in, type your password and click the **Sign In** button.

7 If you want to leave your previous e-mail address as the primary one and your new e-mail address as secondary, close the Add & change e-mail address box.

8 If you want to make your new e-mail address the primary one, click the **Make primary** link next to it.

9 If you want to remove your previous e-mail address, click the **Remove** link next to it.

10 Click **Close.**

11 If you want to continue editing your profile, hover over the **Profile** menu and click **Edit Profile.**

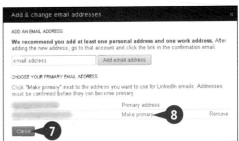

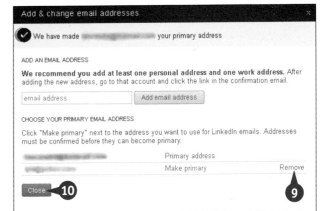

TIP

Which e-mail addresses should I add to my LinkedIn account?
You may want to add one business and one personal address, with the personal one as your secondary address.

Add, Remove, or Revise a Position

You can add a new job position to your profile as well as remove an existing one. You can also easily revise a position if you want to add or modify it. Finally, you can switch the order of two positions that are ongoing or have the same ending date.

Add, Remove, or Revise a Position

1 To add a position in Profile edit mode, move to the Experience section and click the **Add a position** link.

2 Type the information for **Company Name, Title, Location, Time Period,** and **Description.**

3 Click **Save.**

4 To remove a position from your profile, click the **Edit** button next to your job title for the position.

5 Scroll to the bottom of the listing for that position, and click the **Remove this position** link.

LinkedIn displays a message asking if you are sure you want to remove this position.

6 Click **Yes, remove** to confirm that you want to remove it.

LinkedIn removes the position from your profile.

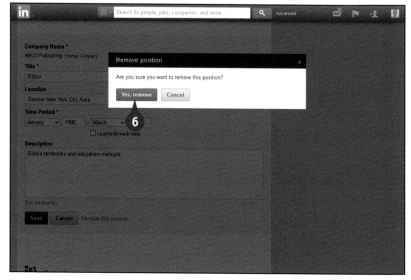

7 To revise a position, click the **Edit** button next to that position.

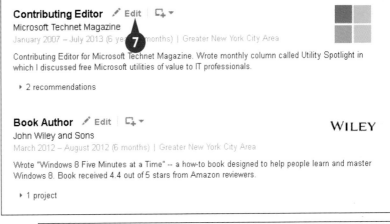

Contributing Editor ✏ Edit ⬚ ▾
Microsoft Technet Magazine
January 2007 – July 2013 (6 years, 7 months) | Greater New York City Area

Contributing Editor for Microsoft Technet Magazine. Wrote monthly column called Utility Spotlight in which I discussed free Microsoft utilities of value to IT professionals.

▸ 2 recommendations

Book Author ✏ Edit ⬚ ▾
John Wiley and Sons
March 2012 – August 2012 (6 months) | Greater New York City Area

Wrote "Windows 8 Five Minutes at a Time" -- a how-to book designed to help people learn and master Windows 8. Book received 4.4 out of 5 stars from Amazon reviewers.

▸ 1 project

8 Type the new information, and click **Save.**

9 To change the order of two positions, look for a double vertical arrow (⬍) next to your title on both positions. Hold and drag the arrow above or below the other position.

LinkedIn changes the order of the two positions.

Note: The arrow appears only next to two positions that are still ongoing.

Company Name *
Microsoft Technet Magazine   Change Company | Edit Display Name

Title *
Contributing Editor

Location
Greater New York City Area

Time Period *
January ▾ 2007 – July ▾ 2013
☐ I currently work here

Description
Contributing Editor for Microsoft Technet Magazine. Wrote monthly column called Utility Spotlight in which I discussed free Microsoft utilities of value to IT professionals.|

See examples

[Save] [Cancel] Remove this position

Webmaster and Web Developer ✏ Edit ⬚ ▾ ⬍
The NeuGroup
November 2006 – Present (7 years 4 months)

I work as a consultant for The NeuGroup - www.neugroup.com, a firm that establishes peer groups for treasury executives and publishes a monthly newsletter called iTreasurer.

TIP

How does LinkedIn normally sort my job positions?
LinkedIn automatically sorts your job positions starting with the most recent and then going back in time, the same order you would use on your resume.

Revise Your Education

Need to correct or add certain details about your education? You can revise the name, dates, degree, field of study, grade, and other items listed for any of your schools.

Revise Your Education

1. To revise your education in Profile edit mode, move to the Education section and click the pencil icon (⬚) or the word **Edit** to the right of your school name.

2. To change the name of the school, click the link to **Change School** and start typing the name. Select the school from LinkedIn's list if it appears. Otherwise, continue typing the name of your school.

3. To revise the dates attended, click the arrows (⬚) under **Dates Attended** and change the start and end years (or expected graduation year).

4. To change your degree, delete the existing degree and start typing the new degree name in the **Degree** field. Select your degree from LinkedIn's list if it appears. Otherwise, continue typing the name of your degree.

5. To revise your field of study, delete the existing field and type the new one in the **Field of Study** field.

6. To change your grade, type the new one in the **Grade** field.

7. To add or revise your activities or school clubs, type the information in the **Activities and Societies** field.

8. To add more details about your school or education, type them in the **Description** field.

9. Click **Save.**

10 To move your education higher or lower in your profile, hold your mouse down over the double vertical arrow (⬍) to the right of the **Add education** link.

11 Drag the double vertical arrow (⬍) higher or lower on the page to move the Education section and release your mouse to drop the section in its new positon.

12 Click the **Done editing** button when you are finished editing your profile.

TIP

Can I move other sections of my profile to a different position?
Yes, you can move the position of your summary, Skills & Endorsements, Publications, Projects, and any other section in which you see the double vertical arrow, thus helping you sort your overall profile in your own preferred order.

Those of you with Facebook or Twitter accounts can easily spread the word about your LinkedIn profile to your friends and followers. You simply *share* a link to your profile through either of the two social networks. Sharing your profile through social media is a helpful way to promote it, both after you initially create it and after you make any major changes to it.

Share Your Profile on Facebook or Twitter

1 Open your profile page if it is not already open.

2 Hover over the drop-down arrow (▾) next to the **Edit Profile** button, and click **Share profile**.

LinkedIn displays a Share window with default text that links to your LinkedIn profile.

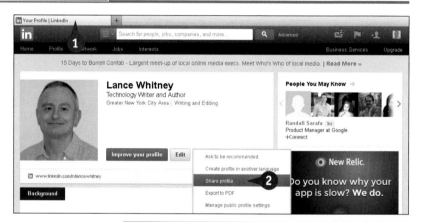

3 Revise the default text in the text field if you want to change it.

Note: Do not change the link to your LinkedIn profile.

4 To share your profile on Facebook, click the Facebook icon.

LinkedIn displays a window asking you to log into your Facebook account.

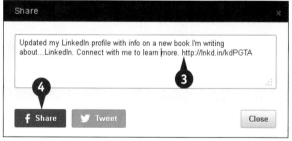

5 Type your Facebook password in the **Password** field, and click the **Log In** button.

A Log in with Facebook window appears, asking for your permission to grant LinkedIn access to some of your Facebook profile information.

6 Click **Okay.**

A second Log in with Facebook window appears, asking for permission to post to Facebook.

7 Click **Okay.**

LinkedIn posts your shared profile message on Facebook and returns you to the Share window. The Facebook icon now says: "Shared."

8 To share your profile link on Twitter, click the Tweet icon.

LinkedIn displays a window asking for permission to access some of your Twitter information and prompting you to type your Twitter username and password.

9 Type your Twitter username or e-mail address in the **Username or e-mail** field.

10 Type your Twitter password in the **Password** field.

11 Click the **Authorize app** button.

LinkedIn posts your shared profile message on Twitter and returns you to the Share window. The Tweet icon now says: "Tweeted."

12 Click **Close** to close the Share window and return to your profile page.

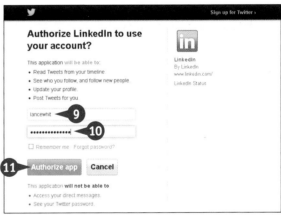

TIPS

Do I have to approve or authorize Facebook and Twitter each time I want to post an update from LinkedIn?
No, after the initial approval or authorization, you can post directly to Facebook or Twitter from then on.

See Who's Viewed Your Profile

How do you know your profile is drawing in viewers? You can see how many people have recently checked out your profile and in some cases find out the names of some of those people. This can help you gauge how successful your profile is at attracting attention.

See Who's Viewed Your Profile

1 Scroll down your LinkedIn home page until you see a section in the right column called Who's Viewed Your Profile.

The section reveals how many people have viewed your profile and how often you have shown up in LinkedIn's search results over a certain number of days.

2 Click the **Your profile has been viewed by x people in the past x days** link.

The Who's viewed your profile page appears. The page displays the accounts of people who have viewed your profile. Some are listed by name, some are listed by title or industry, and some are anonymous.

3 Click the **Search** button next to an account listed by title or industry if you want to see the names of people who may have viewed your profile.

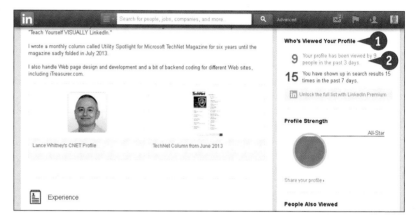

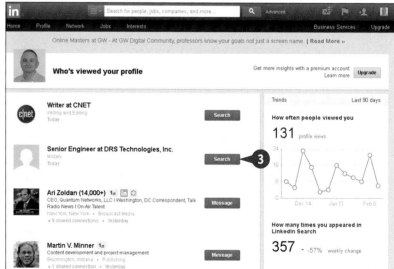

④ Click the **Connect** button next to the name of someone who searched your profile if you want to add that person to your network.

Note: The right column of the Who's viewed your profile page reveals how many people viewed your profile and found you by keywords over the past 90 days. The column also displays the names of keywords that led people to you.

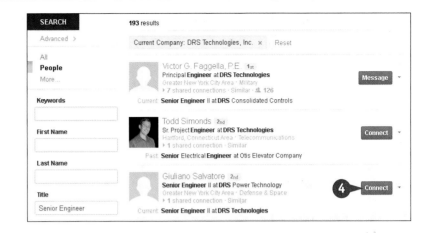

Can I export my profile to a PDF?

If you want a copy of your profile to store on your computer, LinkedIn can help. You can save your profile as an Adobe PDF, giving you the ability to e-mail it, print it, or simply save it as a readable document.

① From your profile page, hover over the drop-down arrow (▾) next to the Edit Profile button, and click **Export to PDF.**

② From the Opening [YourName].pdf window, make sure **Save File** is selected and click **OK.**

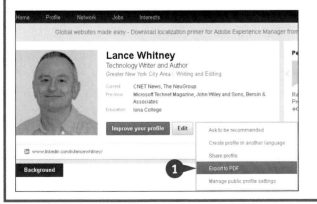

If you receive an Enter name of file to save to... window, select a location for the file on your computer. You can also change the name of the file if necessary. Click **Save.**

Open the folder on your computer in which you saved the PDF, and double-click the file to open it.

Opening the file requires that you have Adobe Reader installed on your computer.

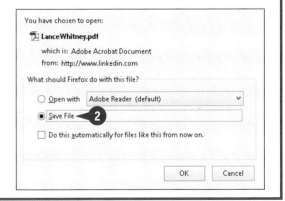

CHAPTER 7

Adding Endorsements and Recommendations

You can bring more power and appeal to your profile by adding skills that can elicit *endorsements* from other people. Such information carries weight because it comes from people who have actually worked with you. You can manage the skills listed on your profile so they can be endorsed by the people in your network, and you can endorse their skills as well. You can also request *recommendations* from people you know and offer them your own recommendations.

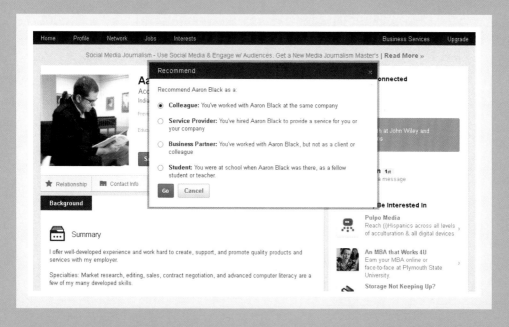

Manage Your Skills

In Chapter 2, you learned how to add your professional skills to your profile. You can manage those skills by adding more, removing ones that no longer apply, and changing the order in which those skills appear. Your goal is to ensure that the skills you feel represent you the best appear in your profile.

Manage Your Skills

1 To set up or add skills to your profile, click the **Profile** menu and then click **Edit Profile.**

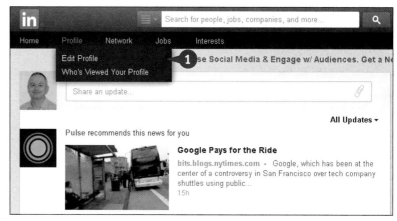

2 Scroll down to the Skills & Endorsements section, and click the pencil icon (✐) or the **Edit** link.

3 In the **What are your areas of expertise?** field, start typing the name of a skill you want to add.

After you type the first character of your skill, LinkedIn displays a list of skills. Continue typing, and LinkedIn narrows the list.

4 Select your skill from LinkedIn's list if it appears. Otherwise, continue typing the name of your skill, and click the **Add** button to add the skill.

Repeat steps **3** and **4** to add more skills.

5 Remove any skill you do not want to appear by clicking the **X** (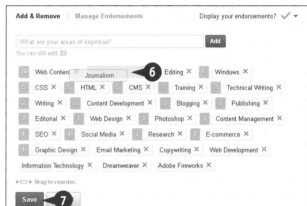) next to it.

6 Reorder your skills by dragging and dropping a specific skill name to another position.

7 Click **Save**.

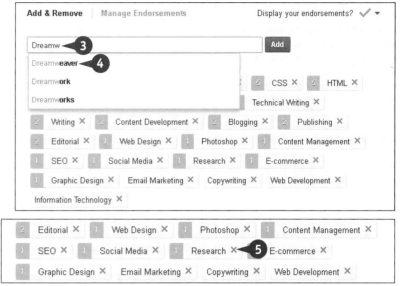

8 Scroll to the top of your profile page, and click the **Done editing** button.

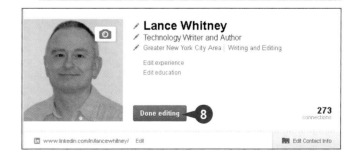

What types of skills should I add to my profile?
You can start off by adding general skills, such as marketing. But be sure to add more specific skills, such as social media marketing, to stand out from the rest of the crowd.

View and Manage Your Endorsements

How do people who view your profile know you actually possess the skills you have listed? Here is where your LinkedIn connections can help. The people who know you can endorse certain skills as a sign that you do in fact possess them. You can then manage those endorsements to highlight specific ones and remove or hide others that you feel may be less relevant to your background.

View and Manage Your Endorsements

1 To view your endorsements, open your profile page and scroll down to the Skills & Endorsements section.

By default, LinkedIn displays your skills based on how many have received the greatest number of endorsements, unless you manually reordered them.

The skills with the greatest number of endorsements appear in the top section. Those with just a few endorsements appear in the bottom section.

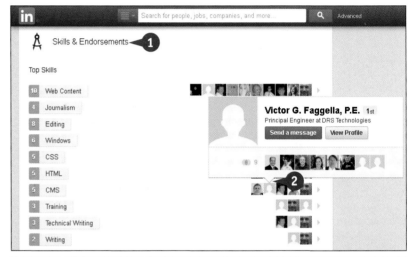

2 Hover over each of the thumbnail photos next to a skill to see the name of each person who endorsed it.

As you hover over a thumbnail photo, the name of the person appears with links to send a message or view that person's profile.

3 Click the number in the blue square at the beginning of a thumbnail photo list to see the names of all people who endorsed that particular skill.

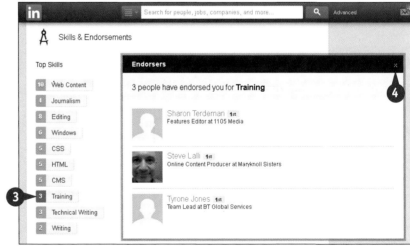

4 Click the **X** (❎) to close the window.

5 Click the name of a specific skill to search for jobs looking for that skill.

LinkedIn displays a page of search results with jobs related to that skill.

Click your browser's back button to return to your profile page.

6 Scroll to the top of your profile page and click the **Edit** button. Scroll back down to the Skills & Endorsements section and click the pencil icon or **Edit** link.

7 Click the **Manage Endorsements** link.

8 If you want to remove all your endorsements, click the **Display your endorsements** arrow and change the setting to **No, do not show my endorsements.**

9 Otherwise, click a specific skill.

LinkedIn displays a list of the people who endorsed that skill.

10 Click the check box (☑ changes to ☐) next to the names of any people whom you do not want to appear as endorsers.

11 Click the **Show/hide all endorsements** check box (☑ changes to ☐) to show all the names of the endorsers for that skill.

Click the **Show/hide all endorsements** check box (☐ changes to ☑) again to hide all the names.

Click **Save** when you are finished.

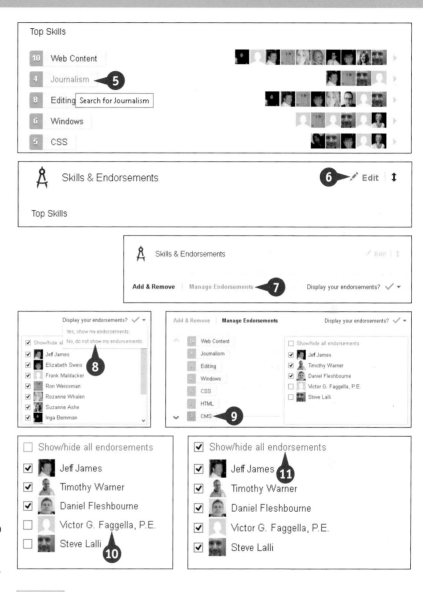

TIP

Does an endorsement really help?
Endorsements are quick and easy to add, so they do not carry as much weight as recommendations. But they still serve to highlight your skills based on the feedback of other people.

Endorse Other People

One of the benefits to a professional network like LinkedIn is that you can help other people just as they can help you. As such, you can endorse the skills of people whom you know professionally.

Endorse Other People

1 From any LinkedIn page, click the **Network** menu and then click **Contacts.**

2 At the Contacts page, click the name of a contact you want to endorsement.

LinkedIn displays that person's profile page with an **Endorse** button in the top section.

3 Click the **Endorse** button.

LinkedIn displays a blue window that lists several of the person's skills.

4 Click the **X** (⊠) next to any skill you do not want to endorse.

5 Start typing the name of a new skill you want to endorse in the **Type another area of expertise** field. Click the skill from LinkedIn's list of suggestions if it appears. Otherwise, finish typing it.

6 Click the **Endorse** button to endorse the listed skills.

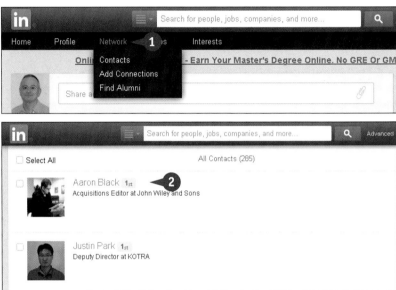

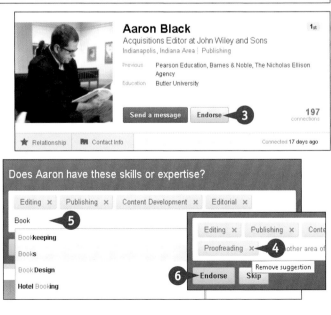

LinkedIn displays another window asking you to endorse the skills of other people in your network.

7 Click the **Endorse** link for any person if you want to endorse the specific skill listed.

As you endorse one person, another person appears.

8 Click **View more** to refresh the list.

9 Click the **Close** button to turn off the endorsement window.

10 To manage your endorsements for your current contact, scroll down the profile page until you see the Skills & Endorsements section.

Hover over the plus sign (☐) next to the specific skill that you want to endorse. The word **Endorse** appears next to the plus sign.

11 Click the plus sign to endorse that skill.

12 To remove one of your endorsements, hover over the plus sign next to the skill that you endorsed.

The plus sign turns into a minus sign (⊟) and displays the words **Remove Endorsement.**

Click the minus sign.

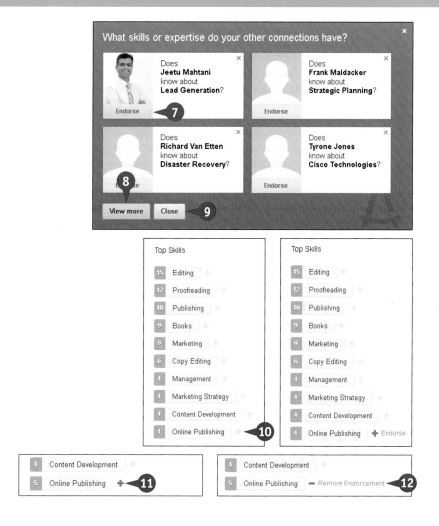

TIP

How many endorsements can I give to someone?
You can give a person as many endorsements as you want, but try to focus on the skills you feel are the most relevant and accurate.

Ask for Recommendations

You can further enhance your profile by requesting recommendations from people you know. A recommendation is similar to a reference that you might ask of someone when you apply for a job. A recommendation gives weight to your profile because people can read positive comments about you from coworkers, employers, and others in your network.

Ask for Recommendations

1 To open the recommendations page, click the **Profile** menu to load your profile.

2 Hover your mouse over the down arrow to the right of the **Edit** button, and click the link for **Ask to be recommended.**

LinkedIn displays the Ask for recommendations page.

3 In the What do you want to be recommended for? section, click the **Choose** arrow and select the job or school for which you want to be recommended.

Note: You can also add a new job or school for this page by clicking the appropriate link in the **[Add a job or school]** line.

4 In the Who do you want to ask? section, start typing the name of the person from whom you would like the recommendation.

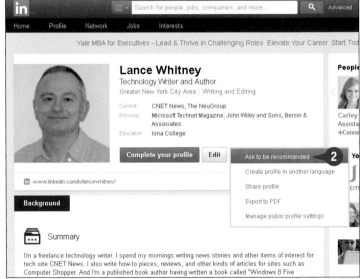

LinkedIn displays the name of the person based on the first few letters you type.

5 Select the name from LinkedIn's list.

6 Under the Create your message section, confirm or revise the subject line, and then confirm or revise the body of the request.

7 Click **Send**.

LinkedIn returns you to the home page with a message that your request for a recommendation has been sent.

Note: Your recipient receives the request as an e-mail.

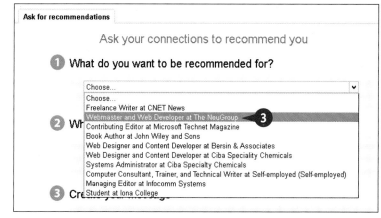

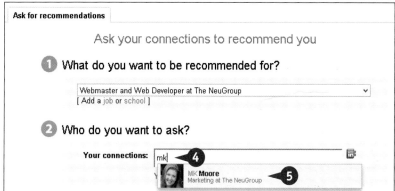

TIP

How can I increase the chances of receiving a recommendation?

Avoid using the generic subject and body of the request. Instead, personalize the subject and body of your message to gear them specifically to your recipient.

Make a Recommendation

Just as your LinkedIn connections help you by providing recommendations, you can help them in the same way. As such, you should make an effort to provide recommendations to colleagues and coworkers where you feel such recommendations are appropriate and deserved. You can provide a recommendation in response to a person's request or freely offer a recommendation on your own.

Make a Recommendation

Make a Recommendation from Your Contacts Page

1 From any LinkedIn page, click the **Networks** menu and then click **Contacts.**

2 Scroll down your list of contacts until you find the person you want to recommend, or simply search for the specific contact by following the steps in the "View Your Contacts" section of Chapter 3: Building Your Network.

3 Click the name of the person you want to recommend to open his or her profile.

4 Hover your mouse over the down arrow to the right of the **Endorse** button, and click the **Recommend** link.

LinkedIn displays a Recommend window asking how you know the person: **Colleague, Service Provider, Business Partner,** or **Student.**

5 Click the appropriate option
(☐ changes to ☉), and then
click **Go**.

LinkedIn displays a Create
your recommendation form for
you to complete.

Note: The initial fields differ
depending on which of the four
relationships options you choose.

6 If you select **Colleague**, fill out
the Relationship section by
selecting the appropriate
options in the fields for **Basis
of recommendation, Your title
at the time**, and **[Contact's]
title at the time.**

7 If you select **Service
Provider**, fill out the top
section by selecting the
appropriate options in the
fields for **Position you're
recommending [contact] for,
Service category**, and **Year
first hired.** Then click the top
three attributes in the Top
Attributes section.

8 If you select **Business
Partner**, fill out the
Relationship section by
selecting the appropriate
options in the fields for **Basis
of recommendation, Your
title at the time**, and
[Contact's] title at the time.

9 If you select **Student**, fill out
the Relationship section by
selecting the appropriate
options in the fields for **Basis
of recommendation, Your
title at the time**, and
[Contact's] title at the time.

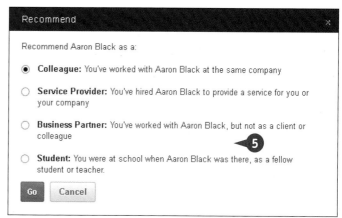

continued ▶

After you select the option that best describes your relationship with the person you want to endorse, you can move on to the next step of writing the endorsement.

Make a Recommendation (continued)

10 After you have filled out the top section, type your recommendation in the **Written Recommendation** field.

Note: Your recommendation can be 3,000 characters maximum, including spaces and paragraph returns.

11 Click the **view/edit** link to revise the recommendation.

12 Read the recommendation, and make any necessary changes to it.

13 You can also customize the message sent to the person being recommended by revising the generic text in the **Personalize this Message** field.

14 Click **Send.**

LinkedIn sends your recommendation to the recipient and brings you back to that person's profile page.

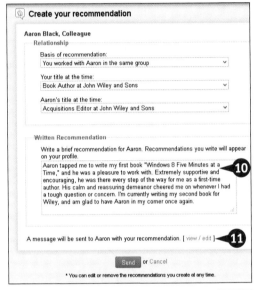

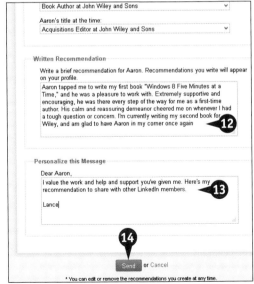

Make a Recommendation in Response to a Request

1 Open your primary e-mail account to view the recommendation request, and click the link in the e-mail to recommend the person.

2 Alternatively, click the e-mail icon in LinkedIn, and click the **View** button to view the person's request.

LinkedIn opens your inbox and displays the recommendation request.

3 Click the **Write Recommendation** button in the e-mail.

LinkedIn displays a recommendation page.

Follow steps **5** to **14** to send the recommendation.

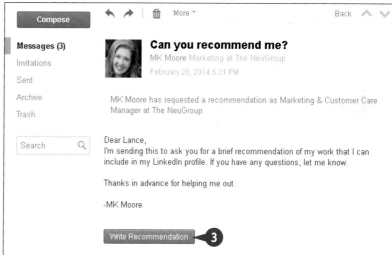

What happens with a recommendation that I write?
The person who receives your recommendation will be able to read it and decide whether or not it should go live.

Manage Your Recommendations

After you have received recommendations, you can opt to show or hide only certain ones. You can also request a revision to a recommendation if you feel that any changes are needed. Your goal is to then ensure that the recommendations that do appear on your profile are relevant and helpful.

Manage Your Recommendations

1 To open the recommendations page, click the **Profile** menu to load your profile.

2 Hover your mouse over the down arrow to the right of the **Edit** button, and click the link for **Ask to be recommended.**

LinkedIn displays the Ask for recommendations page.

3 Click the **Received** link at the top of the page.

LinkedIn displays the Manage recommendations you've received page.

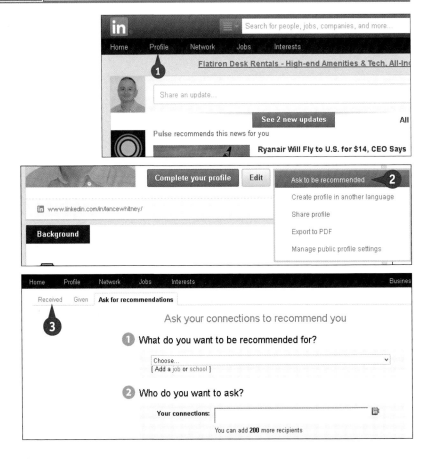

4 Click the **Manage** command next to a recommendation you want to hide.

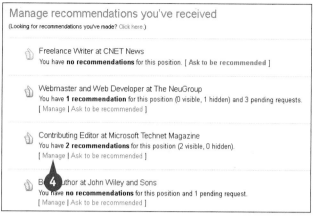

5 Click the **Show** check box (☑ changes to ☐) next to a checked recommendation to hide it.

6 Click the **Save Changes** button.

LinkedIn returns you to the home page.

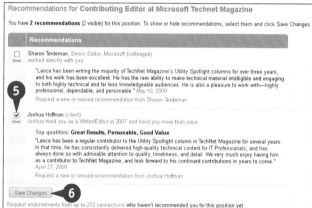

7 Repeat steps **1** to **3** to return to the Received section on the recommendations page.

8 Click the **Manage** command next to a hidden recommendation you want to display.

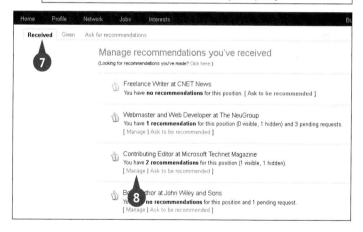

continued ▶

A After you have chosen a recommendation that you want to hide, you can click its check box to turn off the check mark.

Manage Your Recommendations (continued)

9 Click the **Show** check box (☐ changes to ☑) next to the recommendation to display it.

10 Click the **Save Changes** button.

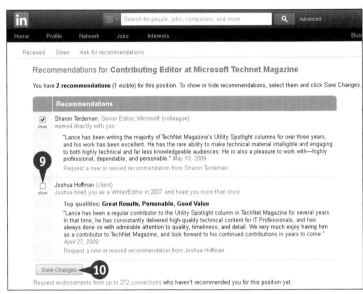

11 Repeat steps **1** to **3** to return to the Received section on the recommendations page.

12 To request a revision to a recommendation, click the **Manage** button next to the recommendation.

13 Click the link to **Request a new or revised recommendation** from the person.

LinkedIn displays the Ask your connections to recommend you form.

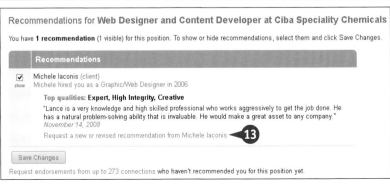

⑭ Revise the subject line and body of the message if necessary.

⑮ Click **Send.**

⑯ To manage a recommendation that you gave, click the **Given** tab.

⑰ At the Manage recommendations you've sent section, click **Edit** for the recommendation you want to change.

⑱ To remove the recommendation, click the link to **Withdraw this recommendation.**

⑲ To edit the recommendation instead, click and change the fields at the top of the form if necessary.

⑳ Revise the recommendation in the **Written Recommendation** field.

㉑ Click **Send.**

TIP

What happens with a recommendation that I revise?
The person who receives the revised recommendation will be able to approve your changes before they go live.

CHAPTER 8

Using Groups

LinkedIn offers virtual *groups* that you can join to network with other people who have the same professional interests, skills, and profession as you do. In a group, you can ask and answer questions and read comments from fellow members, all of which can prove valuable in your professional knowledge and growth.

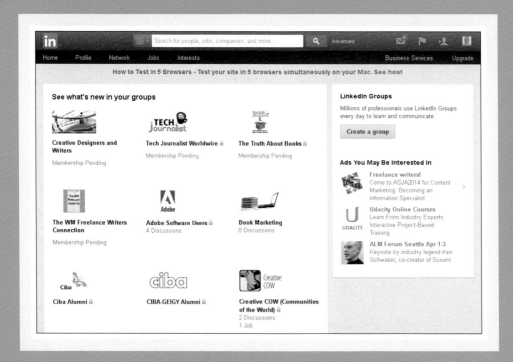

Find a Group

Your first step is to find a group or groups that interest you. You can seek out groups to join by searching for a specific name or a keyword based on a profession, interest, industry, or other item.

Find a Group

1 From any LinkedIn page, click the down arrow (■) to the left of the **Search** field at the top and change the selection to **Groups.**

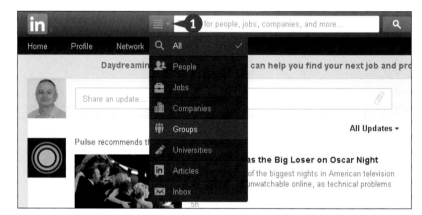

2 In the **Search groups** field, type a name or keyword that refers to a professional interest, such as **web design** or **real estate.**

LinkedIn displays a short list of groups and other items that match your term.

3 Click the search icon (■).

LinkedIn displays a full list of groups that match your search term.

④ Scroll down the page to view the names of the groups.

⑤ Click page 2 and subsequent page numbers to move to the next page of results.

To find relevant groups, you can also look at LinkedIn's suggestions for groups you may like.

⑥ Click the **Home** menu to return to your LinkedIn home page.

⑦ Scroll down the home page until you see a section called Groups You May Like in the right column.

LinkedIn displays the names of three groups that it thinks may interest you based on your professional background.

⑧ Click the **See more** link to see a longer list of groups you may like.

LinkedIn displays a page or multiple pages of groups that it thinks may interest you.

⑨ Review the list of groups.

TIP

How does LinkedIn find groups based on my search term?
LinkedIn looks for instances of your search term in the name and description of all existing groups.

View a Group

You can select a group to view information about it, and in some cases, you can view specific details. The information you see depends on the type of group. Members-only groups show only the names of the members in your network until you join them. Open groups show all relevant details to everyone.

View a Group

① Follow the steps in the previous task to view a list of groups that interest you.

② As you scroll through the list of different groups, notice that some have a small lock icon (🔒) in the description, while others do not have the lock icon.

Note: A lock indicates a members-only group in which posts and discussions are visible only for members. No lock indicates an open group in which posts and discussions are visible to everyone — group members and non-members.

③ Click the name of a members-only group that catches your eye.

The group's non-member page appears.

④ View basic information about the group and see the names of members in your extended LinkedIn network.

When you are finished reading about the group, click your browser's back button to return to the list of groups.

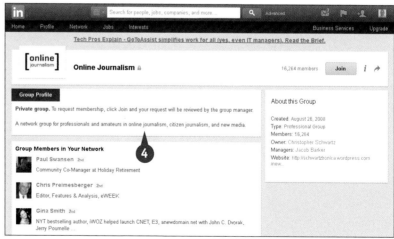

5 Scroll through the list, and click the name of an open group that catches your eye.

The group's full profile page appears, where you can read the group discussions and view other information.

6 Scroll down the Discussions page to view the latest posts and discussion threads.

7 Scroll back to the top of the page, and click the **Promotions** category.

LinkedIn displays the latest promotions.

Note: Group members use promotions to market themselves and their services more appropriately than they can through regular discussions.

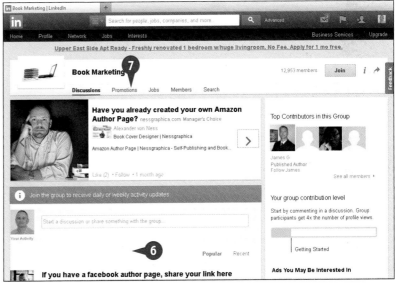

continued ▶

View a Group (continued)

Beyond viewing an open group's discussions and promotion, you can also view its jobs and a list of members.

8 Click the **Jobs** category.

LinkedIn displays a list of jobs, if any, posted in that group.

Note: Some groups are specifically geared for posting jobs. Such groups will often list the word *jobs* in the title or description.

9 Click the **Members** category.

LinkedIn displays a profile and description of the group and a list of all members who are part of your network.

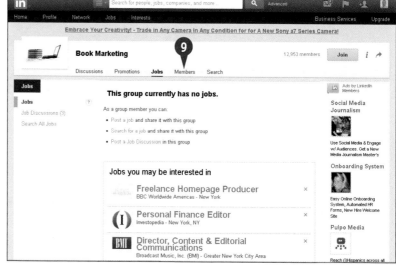

10 Click the Information and settings icon (☐) in the upper right.

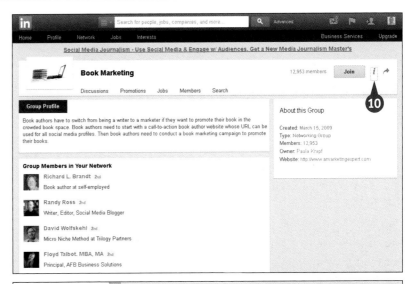

11 Notice further details about the group with links to show you the group profile, group rules, and group statistics.

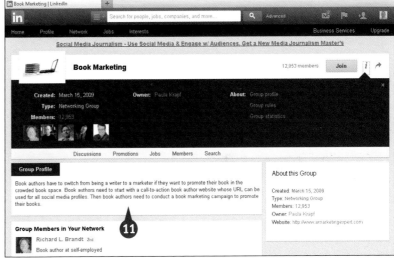

TIPS

Why do some groups display a View button next to them on the search results page, while others display a Join button?
Open groups display a View button because you can view their discussions without having to join. Members-only groups display a Join button because you have to join them to view their discussions.

Can I search for a specific topic in the discussions of a group?
You can search for a topic in an open group. To do so, hover your mouse over the group's View button on the search results page and click the Search Within link to view the group's discussions. From there, you can type a specific word or term in the search field to view discussions related to your topic.

Join a Group

After you have found a group that interests you, the next step is to officially join that group. A members-only group requires that you join to participate in it. An open group allows you to comment on a discussion, but typically you must join to start your own discussions. In some groups, a manager must first approve your request to join. In other groups, your membership becomes immediate as soon as you join.

Join a Group

1 Follow the steps in the previous two tasks to find and view a list of groups that interest you.

2 Click the name of a group that you want to join.

   LinkedIn displays the group's page.

3 Click the **Join** button.

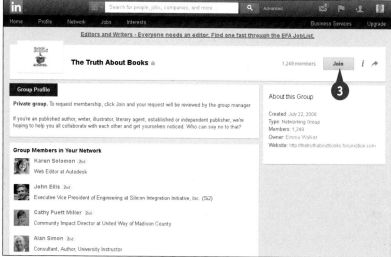

④ Notice that LinkedIn displays a message that your request to join has been received. This message appears only if this is a group that must approve your request to join.

Note: Your request must now be approved by the group's owner or administrator in order for you to become a member. After that request is approved, you will receive an e-mail notifying you that you are now a member of the group.

⑤ Again, follow the steps in the previous two tasks to find and view a list of groups that interest you.

⑥ Click the name of another group that you want to join.

LinkedIn displays the group's page.

⑦ Click the **Join** button.

⑧ Notice that the group displays a welcome message. This message appears only if this is a group that does not need to approve your request to join.

Note: You also immediately receive an e-mail welcoming you to the group.

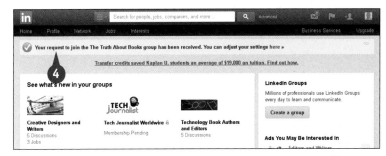

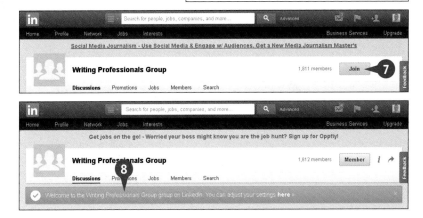

TIP

If a group needs to approve my request to join, can I withdraw my request if I change my mind about joining?
Yes, assuming your request is still pending, you can withdraw your request directly at the group's page.

View Your Groups

You can view all the groups that you have joined or asked to join from a single Groups page. Here you can easily see the name of each group and its current status. You can also change the order in which the groups appear.

View Your Groups

1 From any LinkedIn page, click the **Interests** menu and then click **Groups.**

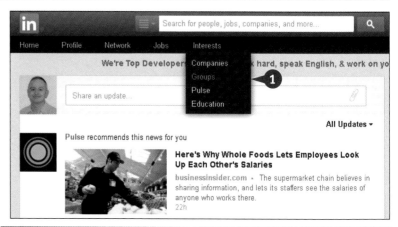

LinkedIn displays a See what's new in your groups page that lists all your groups.

2 View or scroll down the list of groups.

Groups for which you have requested but not yet been granted membership show the status "Membership Pending." Groups of which you are a member may show key details, such as the number of new discussions and jobs.

3 Click a group to open its profile page.

When you finish looking at the group's profile page, click your browser's back button to return to the Groups page.

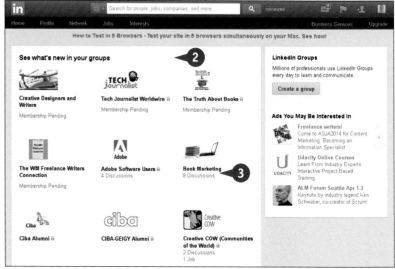

4 To change the order in which the groups appear, click the small account picture in the upper-right corner of the page to display the Accounts & Settings menu.

5 From the Accounts & Settings menu, click the **Review** link for Privacy & Settings.

Type your password at the Sign in to LinkedIn page if required, and click **Sign in.**

6 On the Privacy & Settings page, click the tab for **Groups, Companies & Applications** and then click the link for **Select your group display order.**

7 To move a single group up to the top of the list, click the up arrow next to its name.

The group moves up in the order.

8 To move a group to a specific position, type the number of its new position in the number field.

9 When you are finished, click the **Save changes** button.

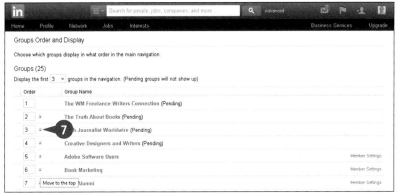

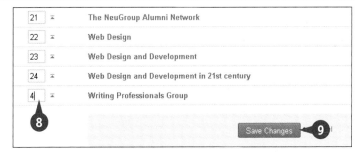

TIP

Are there other places I can see a list of my groups?
Yes. Scroll to the bottom of your profile page, and a list of your groups appears in the Groups section.

Post a Comment or Question

As a group member, you can ask questions and post comments about subjects related to that group, its topic, and other items of interest to members. Asking a question is a key benefit because you tap into the collective knowledge and advice of your fellow group members. Posting a comment in which you share your own knowledge or advice, in turn, helps your fellow members.

Post a Comment or Question

1. From any LinkedIn page, click the **Interests** menu and click **Groups.**

2. Click the group for which you want to post a comment or ask a question.

   The group's page appears.

3. In the **Start a discussion or share something with the group** field, type a title for your comment or question.

4. Type your actual comment or question in the **Add more details field.**

5. Select the type of discussion — **General, Job,** or **Promotion.**

6. Click the **Share** button.

   Your message is either posted immediately or sent to a moderator for review. In the latter case, you will see a message telling you that your post has been submitted for review.

   After the moderator has reviewed your post, it appears live. You will receive a notice by e-mail when your post goes live.

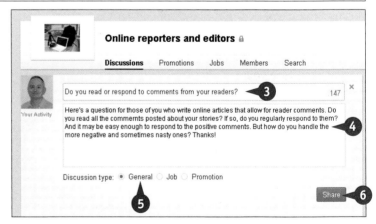

Note: You will also receive e-mail notices if anyone responds to or comments on your post. You can also naturally check the group for any responses to your post.

Respond to a Comment or Question

After you join a group, you will also want to contribute by responding to questions and comments from other people. You can build up your reputation by answering questions posted by your fellow members. Or you can simply add to the discussion by offering your reaction to another person's comment.

Respond to a Comment or Question

1 From any LinkedIn page, click the **Interests** menu and then click **Groups.**

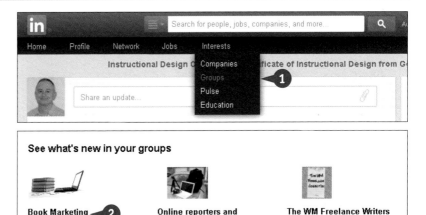

2 Click the group that you want to view.

3 Scroll down the discussions until you find a post to which you want to respond.

4 Click the **Add a Comment** field, and type your comment.

5 By default, you will receive an e-mail when someone adds a comment to this post. But you can disable that option for your current comment by unchecking the **Send me an e-mail for each new comment** box.

6 Click the **Comment** button to post your comment.

Change Your Group Settings

As a group member, you will start to receive e-mails of messages posted to the group in the form of regular *digests*. You can change the frequency with which you receive digests of e-mail for each group. You can also set options to allow the group manager and other members to contact you.

Change Your Group Settings

1 From any LinkedIn page, click the **Interests** menu and then click **Groups** if the Groups page is not already loaded.

2 Click the group that you want to view.

3 Click the Information and settings icon (🛈).

4 In the Information and settings section, click the link for **Your settings.**

⑤ Uncheck the box (☑ changes to ☐) to **Display the group logo on your profile** if you do not want to highlight the group on your profile page.

⑥ Check the box (☐ changes to ☑) to **Send me an e-mail for each new discussion** if you want to receive an e-mail each time a new discussion appears.

Note: Think twice before enabling this setting because it could result in a torrent of e-mails sent to your inbox.

⑦ Uncheck the box (☑ changes to ☐) to **Send me a digest of all activity in this group** if you do not want to receive any e-mail updates from this group.

⑧ If you choose to receive an e-mail digest, click the **Delivery Frequency** arrow (▾) to set the frequency to either daily or weekly.

⑨ Uncheck the box (☑ changes to ☐) to **Allow the group manager to send me an e-mail** if you do not want to receive updates from the manager.

⑩ Uncheck the box (☑ changes to ☐) to **Allow members of this group to send me messages via LinkedIn** if you do not want to be contacted by fellow members.

⑪ Click the **Save changes** button.

You can also change the settings for all your groups in one place.

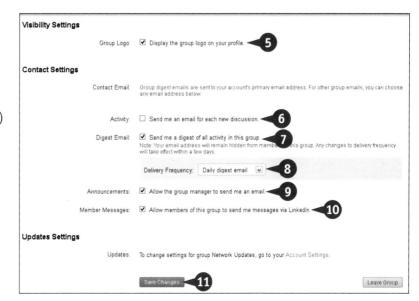

continued ▶

Change Your Group Settings (continued)

12 Click your small account picture in the upper-right corner to display the Accounts & Settings menu.

13 From the Accounts & Settings menu, click the **Review** link for Privacy & Settings. Type your password at the Sign in to LinkedIn page if required.

14 On the Privacy & Settings page, click the tab for **Groups, Companies & Applications** and then click the link for **Set the frequency of group digest e-mails.**

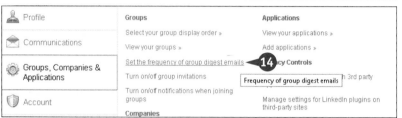

15 In the Frequency of group digest e-mails window, select the frequency for each group, choosing among **Daily Digest E-mail, Weekly Digest E-mail,** or **no E-mail.**

16 Click the **Save changes** button.

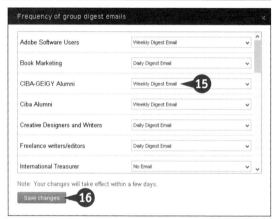

17 To turn group invitations on or off, click the link for **Turn on/off group invitations.**

18 Uncheck the box (☑ changes to ☐) for **I am open to receiving group invitations** if you do not want to receive any invitations to join a group.

19 Click the **Save changes** button.

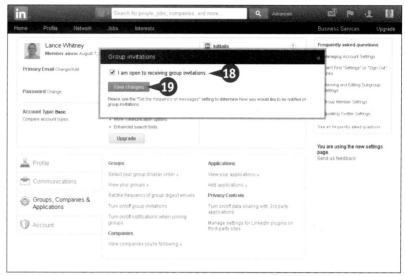

20 To turn notifications on or off when joining groups, click the link for **Turn on/off notifications when joining groups.**

21 If you want to maintain privacy about the groups you join, uncheck the box (☑ changes to ☐) to **Yes, publish an update to my network whenever I join a group that has these notifications enabled by the group owners.**

22 Click the **Save Changes** button.

TIPS

Why would I hide a group logo on my profile page?

If you belong to a lot of groups, you may want to hide some of them to better shine the spotlight on only certain groups.

What would happen if I enable the option to send me an e-mail for each new discussion?

With this option enabled, you receive an e-mail anytime a group member starts a new discussion. This option may be fine for a small group. But an active group could easily trigger dozens of e-mails sent to you each day.

Leave a Group

What happens if a group no longer interests you? You can choose to leave the group if you decide it is no longer relevant to your career, company, or professional interests.

Leave a Group

1 From any LinkedIn page, click the **Interests** menu and then click **Groups.**

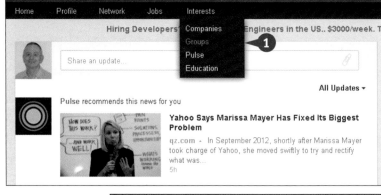

2 Click the name of the group you want to leave.

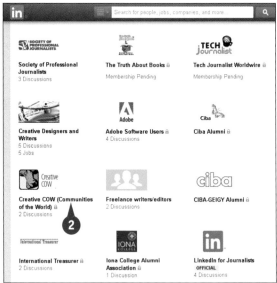

3 Hover over the **Member** button in the upper-right corner.

The button changes to display the word *Leave*.

Click the **Leave** button.

A confirmation message appears asking if you are sure you want to leave the group.

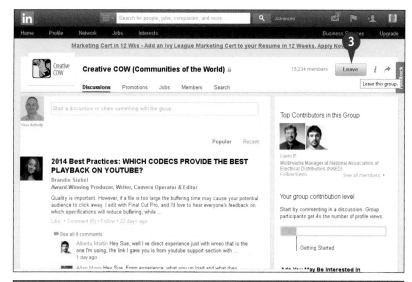

4 Click **Cancel** if you change your mind; otherwise, click **Leave.**

A message appears telling you that you are no longer a member of that group.

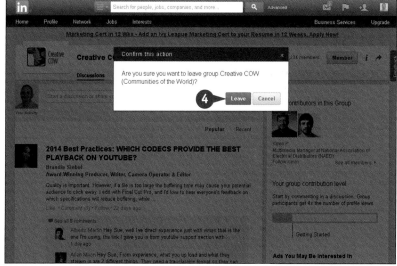

If I needed approval to join a certain group, do I need approval to leave it?

No, you can leave any group without approval or permission required. And no explanation is necessary as to why you want to leave.

Can I rejoin a group after I have left?

Yes, if a group does not require approval to join, you can easily rejoin it at any point. If the group requires approval to join, then your

request to join it again is sent to the group's administrator. If your name stands out, the administrator might wonder why you left and now want to rejoin. But do not let that possibility prevent you from trying to rejoin.

Can I leave a group if my membership is still pending?

Yes, the button for such a group simply says Pending instead of Member. Hovering over the button changes the word to Leave. Clicking the Leave button then withdraws your request to join.

Create a Group

Having trouble finding a group to meet your specific niche? Maybe you should start your own group. And you can do just that. Creating and maintaining your own LinkedIn group requires a certain amount of effort. But if you have the time and drive, it can be a useful way to network with people and enhance your status on LinkedIn.

Create a Group

1. From any LinkedIn page, click the **Interests** menu and then click **Groups.**

2. Click the **Create a group** button in the upper-right corner.

   The group creation page appears with a number of fields for you to complete.

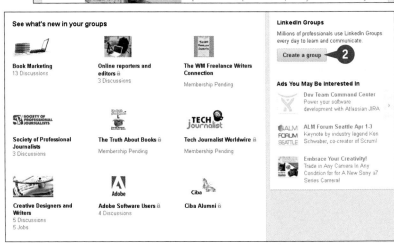

3. To upload a logo or photo to represent your group, click the **Browse** button.

④ Double-click an image from your computer to upload it.

Your logo appears.

Note: Make sure you have the necessary rights to use the image.

⑤ Check the box (☐ changes to ☑) for **I acknowledge and agree that the logo/image I am uploading does not infringe upon any third party copyrights, trademarks, or other proprietary rights or otherwise violate the User Agreement.**

⑥ In the **Group Name** field, type the name of your group.

⑦ In the **Group type** drop-down menu (▾), select the type of group.

⑧ In the **Summary** field, type a brief description of your group.

⑨ In the **Description** field, type a full description of your group.

⑩ In the **Website** field, type a website address for your group if you plan to use one.

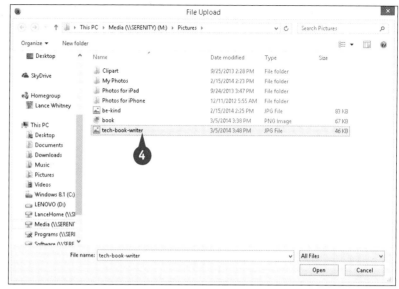

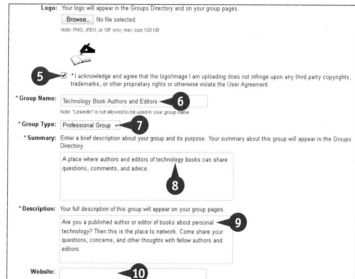

continued ▶

Create a Group (continued)

⑪ In the **Group Owner E-mail** field, confirm or change the e-mail address that you want to use to manage the group.

⑫ In the Access section, click the button (◯ changes to ◉) to set the type of access for your group: **Auto-Join:** Any LinkedIn member may join this group without requiring approval from a manager, or **Request to Join:** Users must request to join this group and be approved by a manager.

⑬ If you select **Auto-Join,** choose which options you want to set by clicking any or all of the following:

Ⓐ Display this group in the Groups Directory.

Ⓑ Allow members to display the logo on their profiles. Also, send your connections a Network Update that you have created this group.

Ⓒ Allow members to invite others to join this group.

⑭ If you select **Request to Join,** choose among the same three options listed above, but also type the name of a domain if you want to pre-approve members with certain e-mail domain(s).

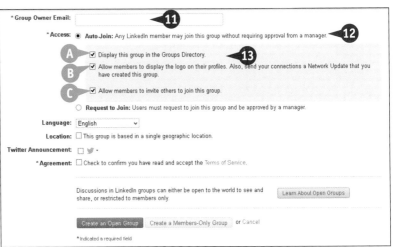

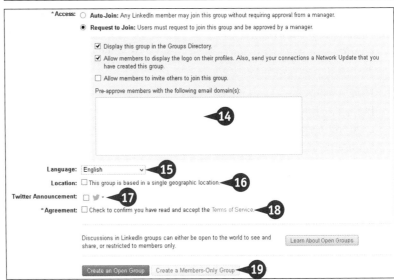

Note: You may want to type a domain for your company if you want to automatically pre-approve all employees.

15 Confirm the language of the group in the **Language** field.

16 Check the **Location** box (□ changes to ☑) if the group is located in a single geographic location, and then choose the country and type the ZIP code of the group.

17 If you already have a Twitter account linked with LinkedIn, check the box (□ changes to ☑) for **Twitter Announcement** and confirm the Twitter account that you want to use to announce the group.

18 In the **Agreement** field, check the box (□ changes to ☑) to confirm you have read and accept the Terms of Service.

19 Finally, click the appropriate button at the bottom to **Create an Open Group** or **Create a Members-Only Group.**

After you create your group, LinkedIn displays a Send Invitations page through which you can invite people to your group.

20 Click **Skip this step.**

Send Invitations

Send invitations to your connections on LinkedIn or even other contacts who are not on LinkedIn. Recipients who accept your invitations will automatically become members of your group.

Connections:

Start typing the name of a connection
Add other email addresses...

* **Subject:**
Lance Whitney invites you to join Technology Book Authors and Editors on LinkedIn

* **Welcome Message:**
I would like to invite you to join my group on LinkedIn. -Lance

Send Invitations or Skip this step **20**

* For our members' protection, group invitations cannot be customized.

TIPS

Does LinkedIn provide instructions on how to manage my group?
After you create your group, LinkedIn sends you an e-mail with a link to a Help Center page on how to manage your group.

Should I create an open group or a members-only group?
You may want to start by creating a members-only group. You can always change that into an open group at a future point.

Invite People to a Group

After you create your own LinkedIn group, as detailed in the previous task, your next step is to invite other people to join. You can invite connections already on LinkedIn and non-LinkedIn members through e-mail.

Invite People to a Group

1 From any LinkedIn page, click the **Interests** menu and then click **Groups.**

2 Select the group you created.

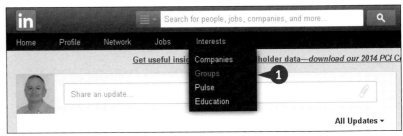

3 On the group's page, click the **Manage** menu.

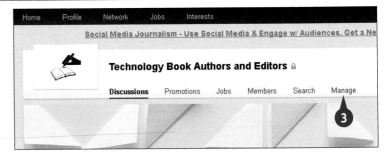

4 On the Manage Group page, click the link to **Send Invitations.**

5 In the **Connections** field of the Send Invitations form, type the name of a LinkedIn connection that you want to invite to the group. Select the person's name from LinkedIn's list.

6 Type and select the name of another connection that you want to invite to the group.

7 To invite someone who is not a LinkedIn member, click the link to **Add other e-mail addresses.**

8 Type the person's e-mail address in the **E-mail Addresses** field.

9 Type another e-mail address if you want to invite another person.

Note: Separate e-mail addresses with commas.

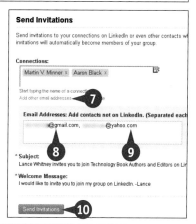

10 Click the **Send Invitations** button.

11 Notice that LinkedIn confirms that you have sent the invitations. You can review the names of the people invited to the group.

Manage People in a Group

How do you manage all the people who want to join your group as well as those who are already members? LinkedIn provides a set of tools just for this purpose. You can pre-approve and approve new members. You can also remove a member from a group and even block the person from trying to rejoin the group.

Manage People in a Group

1 From any LinkedIn page, click the **Interests** menu and then click **Groups.**

2 Select the group you created.

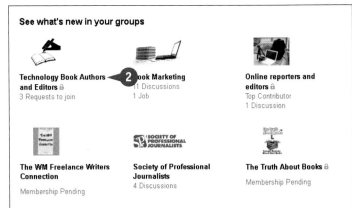

3 On the group's page, click the **Manage** menu.

4 Assuming that your group requires approval before someone can join, click the link to **Pre-approve People.**

5 Type and select the name of a connection that you want to pre-approve.

6 If you want to pre-approve someone who is not yet a LinkedIn member, click the link to **Add other e-mail addresses** and type the e-mail address of the person.

7 Click the **Pre-approve** button.

8 Notice that LinkedIn displays a message telling you that you have successfully pre-approved the number of people you listed.

Again, assuming that your group requires approval before someone can join, you also need to approve or decline requests from people to join your group.

9 Click the **Requests to Join** link.

LinkedIn offers three options: **Approve** (which grants the person's request to join); **Decline** (which denies the person's request to join); and **Decline and Block** (which denies the request and prevents the person from attempting to join in the future).

10 Check the box (☐ changes to ☑) for someone you want to approve, and click the **Approve** link below the person's name.

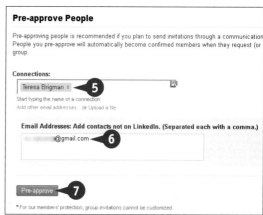

continued ▶

Manage People in a Group (continued)

As you review requests to join your group, you can approve, decline, or decline and block each individual request.

Manage People in a Group (continued)

11 Check the box (☐ changes to ☑) for someone whose request you want to decline, and click the **Decline** link below the person's name.

12 Check the box (☐ changes to ☑) for someone you want to decline and block, and click the **Decline & Block** link below the person's name.

Note: The **Add Note** option sends a note to any managers of the group alerting them to the status of users requesting to join the group. The **Send Message** option sends a note to the manager of the group, which is typically the owner.

13 Click the **Members** tab to view all current members of the group.

14 To remove a member from the group, check the box (☐ changes to ☑) for that member and click the **Remove** button.

Note: You can also block or block and delete a member. **Block** removes the member from the group and prevents that person from trying to rejoin. **Block & Delete** does the same thing but it also deletes all of their past posts and other contributions to the group.

15 To change posting permissions for a member, check the box (☐ changes to ☑) for that person.

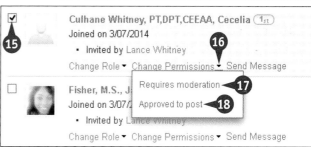

16 Click the **Change Permissions** down arrow (☑).

17 To require that a person's post be approved by a moderator before it goes live, click the **Requires moderation** link.

18 To enable the person to post a message without requiring a moderator's approve, click the **Approved to post** option.

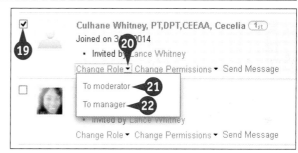

19 To change a member's role, check the box (☐ changes to ☑) for that person.

20 Click the **Change Role** down arrow (☑).

21 To assign that person the role of moderator, click the **To moderator** link.

22 To assign that person the role of manager, click the **To manager** link.

TIP

How can I approve or change roles for multiple members in one shot?

You can check the box for each member that you want to include or check the top box to select all members listed. You then click the appropriate button (Approve, Change Role, and so on) above the list of names to apply that action to all of the checked individuals.

Send a Group Announcement

Have a message you want to send to all members of your group? You can easily do that through a group *announcement*. Creating an announcement sends an e-mail to all members and posts the announcement as a discussion. You can send up to one announcement per week.

Send a Group Announcement

1 From any LinkedIn page, click the **Interests** menu and select **Groups,** assuming the page for your group is not already open.

2 Click the name of your group.

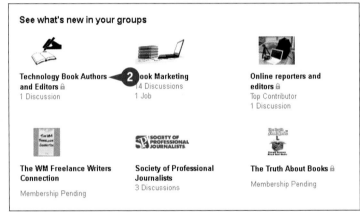

3 On your group's page, click the **Manage** menu.

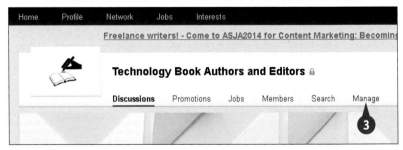

④ Click the **Send an Announcement** link.

The Send an Announcement form opens.

⑤ In the **Subject** field, type a short subject to describe the announcement if you want to revise the generic subject.

⑥ In the **Message** field, type the message you want to announce.

⑦ To receive notifications of comments to your announcement, check the box (☐ changes to ☑) to **Follow this announcement.**

⑧ To highlight the announcement on the group's page, check the box (☐ changes to ☑) to make the announcement a featured discussion.

⑨ Click the **Send Test** button to send a test of the announcement to your own e-mail address.

A message tells you that your test announcement e-mail was sent successfully.

Check your e-mail to view the test announcement.

⑩ On the Send an Announcement page in LinkedIn, click the **Send Announcement** button to send and post the announcement to your group's page.

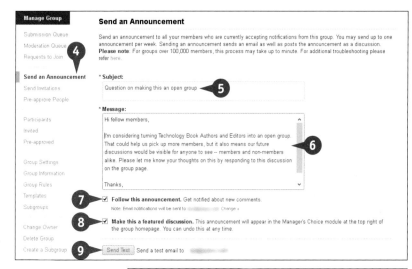

TIP

How do I view my announcement?
Open your Group's Discussions page and click the Recent link above the first discussion. Scroll down the page to read your announcement.

Edit Group Information

You chose all the basic information and settings for your group when you created it. But that does not mean you are stuck with those settings. You can change the group's name, description, website link, and other key information at any time.

Edit Group Information

1 From any LinkedIn page, click the **Interests** menu and select **Groups,** assuming the page for your group is not already open.

2 Click the name of your group.

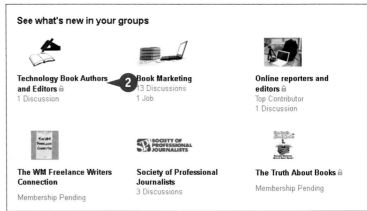

3 On your group's page, click the **Manage** menu.

4 On the Manage Group page, click the **Group Information** link.

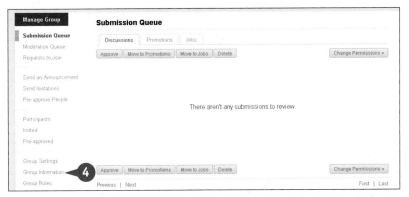

5 To upload a group logo, click the **Browse** button in the Group Logo section.

Note: The image you use for a group logo must be a PNG, JPG, or GIF file with dimensions up to 100 pixels by 50 pixels and a size no larger than 100 KB.

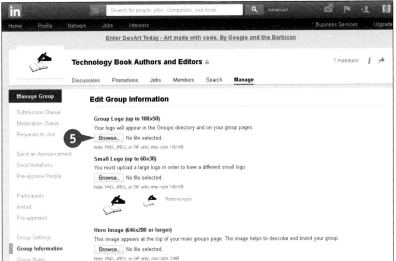

6 From the File Upload window, browse to and double-click the image you want to use for the group logo.

The group logo appears next to the small logo, which you should have set when you initially created your group.

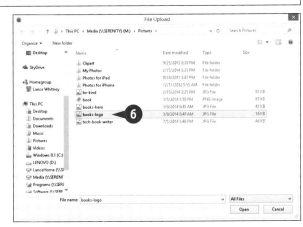

continued ▶

A s you upload the different images for your group, you can see them displayed on the Group Information page.

Edit Group Information (continued)

7 To upload a Hero image, click the **Browse** button in the Hero Image section.

Note: The Hero image must be a PNG, JPG, or GIF file with dimensions at least 646 pixels by 200 pixels and a size no larger than 2 MB.

8 From the File Upload window, browse to and double-click the image you want to use for the Hero image.

LinkedIn displays a Crop Hero image window if the image needs to be cropped.

9 In the Crop Hero image window, crop the image by moving the large yellow rectangle to the appropriate spot.

10 Click **Save**.

The Hero image appears at the bottom of the Hero Image section.

Hero Image (646x200 or larger)
This image appears at the top of your main groups page. The image helps to describe and brand your group.

Browse... **7** selected.

Note: PNG, JPEG, or GIF only; max size 2 MB

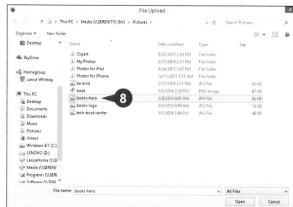

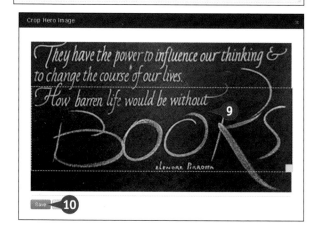

11 Scroll down the page to see the next several settings.

12 Check the box (☐ changes to ☑) for **I acknowledge and agree that the logo/ image I am uploading does not infringe upon any third party copyrights, trademarks, or other proprietary rights or otherwise violate the User Agreement.**

13 Change the name of your group in the **Group Name** field if you want to change it.

14 Change the group type in the **Group Type** drop-down field (☑) if you want to change it.

15 Change the brief description of the group in the **Summary** field if you want.

16 Scroll down the page to see the last few settings.

17 Change the description of the group in the **Description** field if you want.

18 Add or change the **Website** for the group.

19 Click the **Save Changes** button.

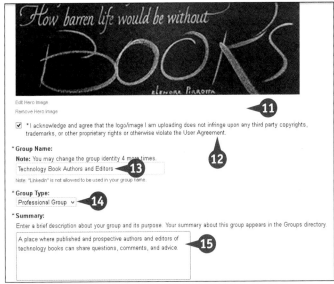

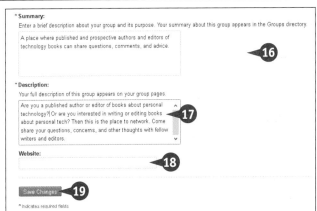

20 Notice that LinkedIn confirms it has updated your group page with the new information.

TIP

Can I change the settings I selected when I first created my group?
Yes. At the page to manage your group, click the **Group Settings** link to change permissions, restrictions, and membership rules. Click the **Group Information** link to change the name, description, logos, and related information.

Create a Subgroup

Want to create a separate group to focus on a specific topic? Instead of launching a brand new group, you can simply set up a *subgroup* from your existing one. A subgroup is devoted to a specific topic or conversation among a smaller number of members of the group.

Create a Subgroup

1 Make sure the Manage Group page for your group is open.

2 Click the link to **Create a subgroup.**

3 On the Create a Subgroup form, follow steps **4** to **18** in the section "Create a Group" in this chapter to fill out the form.

Note: You will see some minor differences between creating a group and creating a subgroup. A subgroup offers a third option for access called **Invite Only,** through which only members you invite are able to join. A subgroup does not display a **Twitter** box for you to announce it to your Twitter followers.

4 Scroll down further in the page to set the next batch of options.

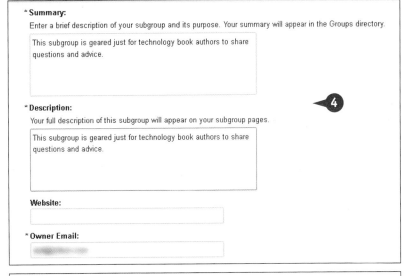

5 When you are finished, click the **Create Subgroup** button.

Note: You can manage and modify the settings for a subgroup using options similar to those for the parent group.

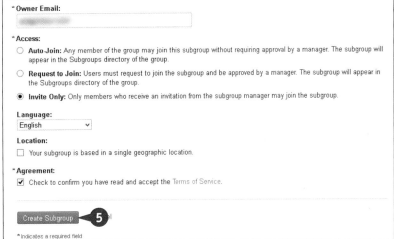

TIPS

Does someone need to be a member of the main group to join the subgroup?
No. Anyone can join or request to join, including people who are not already members of the main group. However, you can set up an auto-join option so that members of the main group can automatically join without requiring approval.

How can people who are not members of the main group find my subgroup?
When you create the membership settings, you can opt to display the subgroup in LinkedIn's Groups Directory so that people can more easily find it.

Make a Members-Only Group an Open Group

You may want to start your group as a members-only group so that only members can view the posts and discussions. But if you want to expand the reach of your group and attract more members, you can change it into an open group. In an open group, anyone can view the discussions and the full details about the group.

Make a Members-Only Group an Open Group

1 Make sure the Manage Group page for your group is open.

2 Assuming your group is members-only, click the **Group Settings** link.

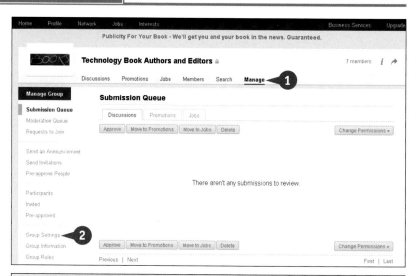

3 Click the button to **Learn About Open Groups.**

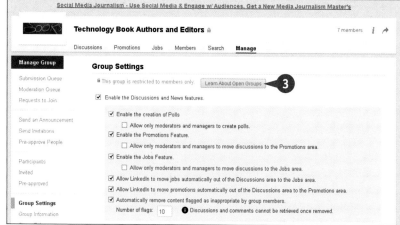

LinkedIn displays a window to explain the differences between an open group and a members-only group.

4 To convert your members-only group into an open group, Click the **I'm interested** button.

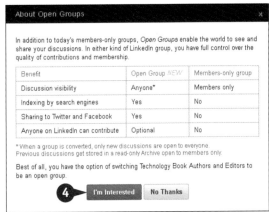

LinkedIn displays another window to explain what will happen after you make your group open.

5 Click the **Switch to Open Group** button.

Note: If you convert a members-only group to an open group, you cannot change it back to a members-only group.

LinkedIn converts your group into an open one and invites you to send an announcement to all group members.

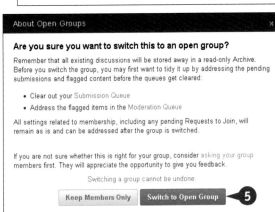

6 Review the announcement and click the **Send Announcement** button to send it to all members.

How do I make sure all the settings are appropriate for an open group?

After you send the announcement, LinkedIn displays a link to Modify your Group's Settings. Click that link to review and revise any setting.

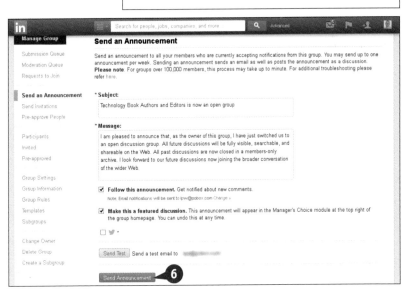

CHAPTER 9

Upgrading Your Free Account to Premium

LinkedIn offers a healthy array of features through the free basic account. But those of you who need more can certainly look into one of the many options for a paid *premium* account. LinkedIn breaks down its premium accounts into four categories: Premium, For Recruiters, For Job Seekers, and For Sales Professionals. Each category offers its own benefits and price levels. This chapter assumes that you currently have a free basic account.

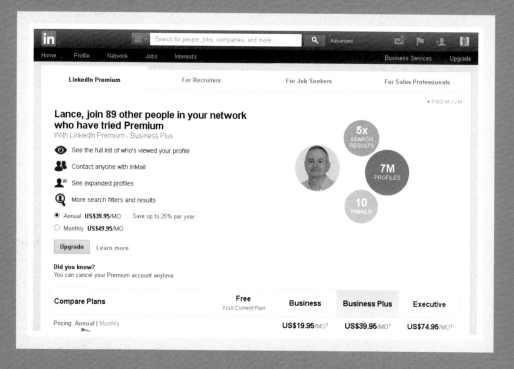

Review LinkedIn's Business Plans

LinkedIn's Business plans provide an extra level of features appropriate for most professionals who feel they need the premium boost. These plans provide new benefits, such as free InMail messages, and greater flexibility to some of the benefits already available with a free account. LinkedIn offers three types of business plans: Business, Business Plus, and Executive.

Review LinkedIn's Business Plans

1. From any LinkedIn page, hover over your profile photo in the upper-right corner.

2. Click the **Upgrade** link for the Account: Basic setting.

   LinkedIn opens a page with tabs for the four different premium options, with the tab for the Business plans the active one. The three business plans are detailed in a comparison chart.

3. Read the information at the top to view some of the basic benefits and the monthly cost of the highlighted option.

4. Click the **Learn more** link to see more information on the Business, or Premium, plans.

   LinkedIn opens a "See what LinkedIn Premium can do for you" page in a new browser tab or window that describes the benefits in greater detail.

5 Scroll down the page slightly to view all of the benefits.

6 Close the "See what LinkedIn Premium can do for you" page to return to the plan comparison page.

7 Scroll down the page if necessary to focus on the Visibility section.

LinkedIn describes and compares the following benefits among the three different Business plans:

A **Who's Viewed Your Profile.**

B **Full Profiles.**

C **Full Name Visibility.**

8 Scroll down to the Reach section.

LinkedIn describes the following three benefits:

D **InMail Messages.**

E **Introductions.**

F **OpenLink.**

9 Scroll further down the page to the Search section.

LinkedIn describes four benefits:

G **Premium Search.**

H **Profiles Per Search.**

I **Saved Search Alerts.**

J **Reference Search.**

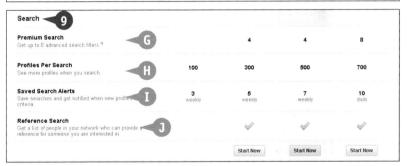

Compare Plans	Free Your Current Plan	Business	Business Plus	Executive
Pricing: Annual | Monthly Save up to 25%		US$19.95/MO[1] Billed annually Start Now	US$39.95/MO[1] Billed annually Start Now	US$74.95/MO[1] Billed annually Start Now
Visibility 7				
Who's Viewed Your Profile — A Unlock the list and see how they found you.		Limited	✓	✓
Full Profiles — B See full profiles of everyone in your network - 1st, 2nd and 3rd degree		Limited Up to 2nd Degree	✓	✓
Full Name Visibility — C See full names of 3rd degree and group connections.				✓
Reach 8				
InMail Messages — D Send direct messages to anyone on LinkedIn. Response guaranteed.[2]		3 per month	10 per month	25 per month
Introductions — E Get introduced to inside sources at companies through LinkedIn connections.	5	15	25	35
OpenLink — F Let anyone on LinkedIn message you for free.[3]		✓	✓	✓
Search 9				
Premium Search — G Get up to 8 advanced search filters.[4]		4	4	8
Profiles Per Search — H See more profiles when you search.	100	300	500	700
Saved Search Alerts — I Save searches and get notified when new profiles match criteria.	3 weekly	5 weekly	7 weekly	10 daily
Reference Search — J Get a list of people in your network who can provide a reference for someone you are interested in.		✓	✓	✓
		Start Now	Start Now	Start Now

TIP

Which premium benefits are the most useful?

That depends on how and why you use LinkedIn. But in general, the Reach benefits may be the most useful because they increase your potential audience of connections and make it easier to connect with people you may not know.

Review LinkedIn's Recruiter Plans

LinkedIn's Recruiter plans are specifically geared toward headhunters, HR personnel, and other professionals who need to match the right people with the right jobs. These plans offer some of the same benefits available through LinkedIn's Business accounts but expand the offerings with tools to help you search for the right talent among the many LinkedIn subscribers. LinkedIn offers three types of Recruiter accounts: Talent Basic, Recruiter Lite, and Recruiter Corporate.

Review LinkedIn's Recruiter Plans

1 Make sure the LinkedIn Premium page is open as described in steps **1** and **2** of the Review LinkedIn's Business Plans section.

2 Click the **For Recruiters** tab.

3 Read the information at the top to view some of the basic benefits and the monthly cost of the highlighted option.

4 Click the **Learn more** link to see more information on the Recruiter plans.

LinkedIn opens a Talent Solutions page describing the benefits in greater detail and offering tips and reports of interest to recruiters.

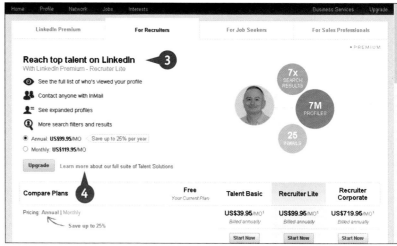

5 Scroll down the Talent Solutions page to view all the information.

6 Click your browser's back button to return to the plan comparison page.

7 Scroll down the page if necessary to focus on the Find and Contact Top Talent section.

LinkedIn describes and compares the benefits among the three different Recruiter plans.

The Find and Contact Top Talent section displays the following benefits: Who's Viewed Your Profile; Full Network Visibility; InMail Messages; and Premium Search, all of which are described in the section "Review LinkedIn's Business Plans."

8 Scroll down to **Recruit Like a Pro.**

LinkedIn describes the following benefits:

A **Recruiting-Specific Design**

B **Pipeline Management**

C **Mobile Access**

D **Company Network**

E **Custom Workflow**

F **Out-of-Network Visibility**

G **Team Collaboration**

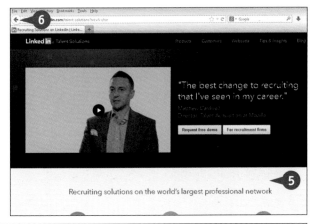

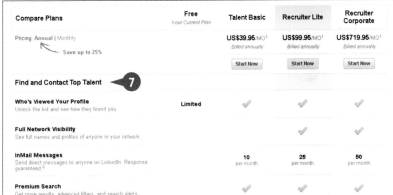

TIP

Does LinkedIn offer any other benefits to recruiters?
LinkedIn offers a free iPhone and Android mobile app called Recruiter that includes several useful features.

Review LinkedIn's Job Seeker Plans

inkedIn's Job Seeker plans are naturally aimed at people looking for work. The benefits are designed to help you track down the right job and make it easier for recruiters to find and notice you. LinkedIn offers three types of Job Seeker accounts: Job Seeker Basic, Job Seeker, and Job Seeker Plus.

Review LinkedIn's Job Seeker Plans

1 Make sure the LinkedIn Premium page is open as described in steps **1** and **2** of the "Review LinkedIn's Business Plans" section.

2 Click the **For Job Seekers** tab.

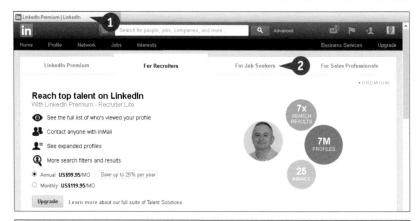

3 Read the information at the top to view some of the basic benefits and the monthly cost of the highlighted option.

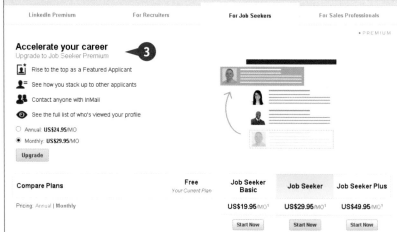

④ Scroll down the page if necessary to focus on the Get in touch section.

LinkedIn describes and compares the benefits among the three different Job Seeker plans.

The Get in touch section displays two benefits: InMail Messages and Who's Viewed Your Profile, both of which are described in the section "Review LinkedIn's Business Plans."

⑤ Scroll down to the Get noticed section.

LinkedIn describes two benefits: Featured Applicant and Premium Badge.

⑥ Scroll down to the Get premium insights section.

LinkedIn describes the following benefits: Applicant Insights, Salary Data, and Job Seeker Group and Webinar.

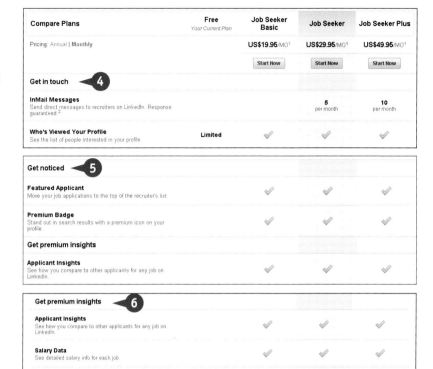

TIP

How else can I used LinkedIn to find a job?
Chapter 10, "Using LinkedIn for Jobs and Business," offers information and advice on using LinkedIn to find a job.

Review LinkedIn's Sales Professional Plans

LinkedIn's Sales Professional plans are geared for sales executives and similar professionals. The goal is to help you find the right leads among your fellow LinkedIn subscribers. LinkedIn offers three types of Sales Professional accounts: Sales Basic, Sales Plus, and Sales Executive.

Review LinkedIn's Sales Professional Plans

1 Make sure the LinkedIn Premium page is open as described in steps **1** and **2** of the Review LinkedIn's Business Plans section.

2 Click the **For Sales Professionals** tab.

3 Read the information at the top to view some of the basic benefits and the monthly cost of the highlighted option.

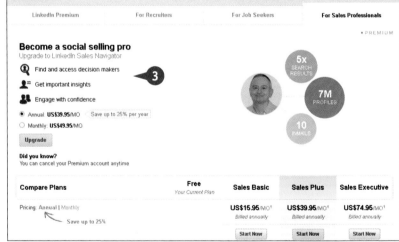

④ Scroll down the page if necessary to focus on the Find Prospects section.

LinkedIn describes and compares the benefits among the three different Job Seeker plans.

The **Find Prospects** section displays three benefits: Search Alerts, Lead Builder, and Premium Search.

⑤ Scroll down to the **Relate with Insight** section.

LinkedIn describes the following benefits: Full Profiles, Who's Viewed Your Profile, and Full Name Visibility.

⑥ Scroll down to the **Engage with Confidence** section:

LinkedIn describes two benefits: Introductions and InMail Messages.

Compare Plans	Free *Your Current Plan*	Sales Basic	Sales Plus	Sales Executive
Pricing: Annual	Monthly Save up to 25%		US$15.95/MO[1] *Billed annually*	US$39.95/MO[1] *Billed annually*	US$74.95/MO[1] *Billed annually*
		Start Now	Start Now	Start Now
Find Prospects ④				
Search Alerts Stay on top of new leads.	3 weekly	5 weekly	7 weekly	10 daily
Lead Builder Manage your pipeline to source and close deals		✓	✓	✓
Premium Search Pinpoint the right leads [2]		4	4	8

Relate with Insight ⑤				
Full Profiles See full profiles of everyone in your network - 1st, 2nd and 3rd degree.	Limited Up to 2nd Degree	✓	✓	✓
Who's Viewed Your Profile Proactively manage inbound queries and interest in your profile.	Limited	✓	✓	✓
Full Name Visibility See full names of 3rd degree and group connections				✓

Engage with Confidence ⑥				
Introductions Get warm introductions to inside sources at companies you're interested in.	5	15	25	35
InMail Messages Gain access to decision-makers. Response guaranteed [3]			10 per month	25 per month
		Start Now	Start Now	Start Now

Looking to buy for your team?

How can I best take advantage of one of LinkedIn's premium sales plans?
LinkedIn's sales plans offer a feature called Sales Navigator that tries to help you generate more leads among your fellow members, reducing the time and energy you might otherwise spend on cold calling.

Sign Up for a Premium Plan

Okay, you have reviewed all the premium plans and have decided to take the plunge and upgrade to one of the paid options. How do you perform this upgrade? The process is relatively simple. You need only fill out a form and provide your credit card information, and your account automatically gets upgraded. Beyond picking the plan itself, the only other choice you need to make is whether you want to pay per month or for an entire year.

Sign Up for a Premium Plan

1 Make sure the LinkedIn Premium page is open as described in steps **1** and **2** of the Review LinkedIn's Business Plans section.

2 Click the tab for the premium option you want to choose — **LinkedIn Premium** (business accounts), **For Recruiters, For Job Seekers,** or **For Sales Professionals.**

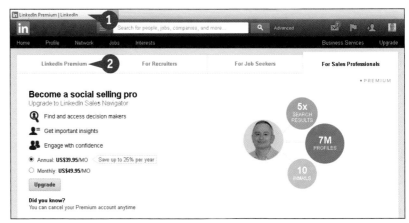

3 Click the button (changes to) to choose either an **Annual** payment or a **Monthly** payment.

4 Scroll to the specific plan that you want, and click the **Start Now** button.

Type your password at the Sign in to LinkedIn page if the page appears.

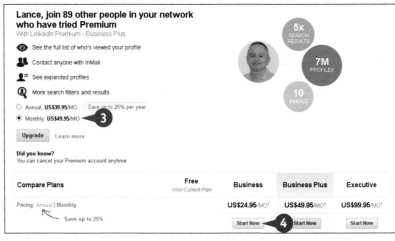

LinkedIn displays a payment information form for you to enter your credit card and billing details.

5 Confirm your name, and enter your credit card information in the **Credit or Debit Card Information** fields.

6 Review or type your name, location, and phone number in the **Billing Information** fields.

7 Click the **Review order** button.

LinkedIn displays a page for you to review your order.

8 Click the check box (☐ changes to ☑) to accept the terms of service.

9 Click the **Place order** button.

LinkedIn processes your payment, and assuming the transaction goes through successfully, brings you to your profile page.

10 Check out some of the features in your premium account.

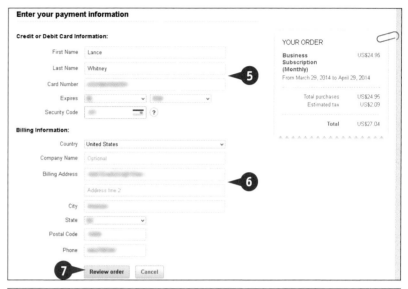

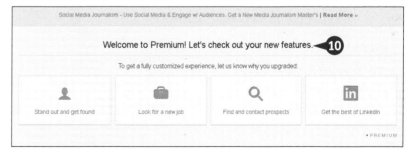

TIP

Can I try out a premium plan before paying for it?
Yes, LinkedIn periodically offers free 30-day trials of certain premium plans. LinkedIn will send you such a promotion via e-mail. Be aware, however, that you still need to enter your credit card information to activate the free trial. You also need to remember to cancel the premium account before the 30 days are up if you do not want to continue it.

Learn to Use Your Premium Plan

How can you learn about all the features and benefits available to you after you purchase a premium plan? LinkedIn provides a way. The site offers a self-guided tutorial that takes you on a tour of your plan's various benefits. You learn enough about each benefit to discover which ones you want to use and just how to use them.

Learn to Use Your Premium Plan

① From any LinkedIn page, hover over your profile picture.

② Click the **Account Tutorial** link for your Account setting.

LinkedIn opens a page offering to help you learn how to use your premium account.

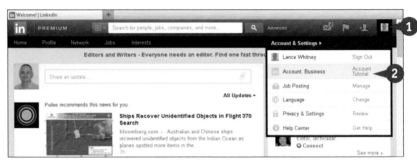

③ Click the **Start tour** link to play a quick video introduction to the tour.

LinkedIn invites you to click any of the icons below the video to get started.

Note: The account tour, features, and information will vary based on which premium plan you purchased.

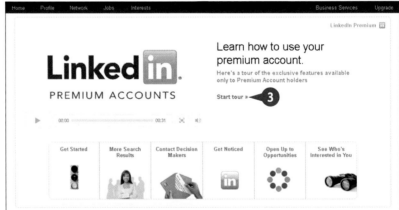

④ Click one of the icons below the video.

LinkedIn explains what the feature is and how to use it.

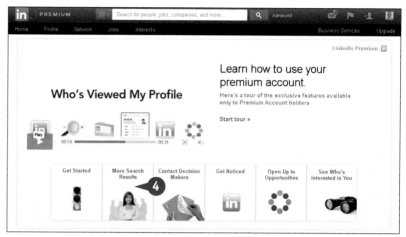

⑤ Click the **Tips** link to view a couple of tips about the feature.

LinkedIn also queues up a video about that feature.

⑥ Click the **Play** button for the video.

LinkedIn plays the video about the feature you selected.

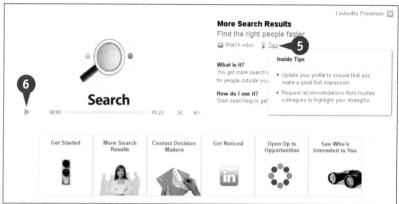

⑦ Click the icon for another feature, click the **Tips** link to view the tips, and click the **Play** button to play the video.

Repeat step **7** for each of the other features.

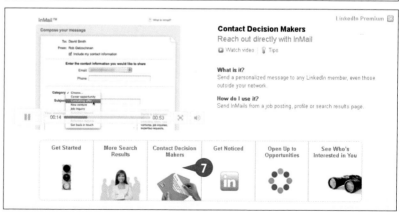

TIP

Can I view these tutorials without signing up for a premium account?
Yes, you can find them at the following webpage: https://www.linkedin.com/static?key=welcome_premium

Use Premium Search

A LinkedIn premium account lends more power to your searches, especially when you search for other members. You can filter your People searches by group, years of experience, seniority level, and several other attributes, all of which can help you narrow the range of people who appear in your results.

Use Premium Search

① From any LinkedIn page, click the down arrow (▣) in front of the search field and click the **People** option to narrow your search to people.

② Type the name of a profession in the search field, and select it from LinkedIn's list of suggestions.

③ Click the magnifying glass icon (▣) to run the search.

LinkedIn displays a list of fellow members who have listed that profession in their profiles.

④ Scroll down the page until you see the search attributes on the left that display the LinkedIn Premium logo next to them.

Note: Depending on your premium plan, not all of the advanced search options will be available to you.

⑤ Click the **Groups** link, and select a group to narrow the search to that specific group.

Note: You can click more than one group.

LinkedIn narrows the search results to show only people from that group or groups.

⑥ Scroll down the page, click the **Interested In** link, and then click an interest to narrow the search to specific professional interests on the part of the people listed.

LinkedIn narrows the search results even further.

continued ▶

After you click on one search option to filter the results, you can view the results or continue to click on more options to filter those results even further.

Use Premium Search (continued)

7 Scroll down the page, click the **Company Size** link, and then click a specific number range to narrow the results based on the size of a person's employer.

LinkedIn again narrows the search results.

8 After you have finished selecting all the advanced search options, scroll down the page to view the results.

9 To remove any of the advanced search parameters, scroll to the top of the page and click the **X** (☒) for the option you want to remove.

10 To remove all the advanced search parameters, click the **Reset** button.

11 Notice that LinkedIn returns to the original search without any of the advanced search options.

Why does LinkedIn display the phrase "Upgrade to access" for some of the advanced search options?

LinkedIn limits certain advanced search options based on the level of your premium plan. With a higher (and more expensive) plan, more options are available to you.

Are the advanced search options available only in the People search?

Most of the advanced search options apply only to the People search, though a Salary option is available in the Jobs search.

How do I know if a certain feature is available only to premium subscribers?

A badge appears next to a feature or option to indicate that it is available only to premium subscribers.

Use OpenLink to Connect with Members

As a LinkedIn premium subscriber, you can now access the OpenLink network. Through this network, you can freely connect with other OpenLink members via InMail, whether they are in your extended network or not. The benefit opens up the number of people that you can add to your network or contact for a specific reason because it does not require an introduction. You can also opt to receive InMail messages from other OpenLink members.

Use OpenLink to Connect with Members

1 From any LinkedIn page, hover over your profile picture.

2 Click the **Review** link for Privacy & Settings.

Type your password, and click the **Sign In** button at the LinkedIn Sign in page.

LinkedIn displays your Privacy & Settings page.

3 In the OpenLink section, click the **Change** link next to the phrase: Not accepting messages.

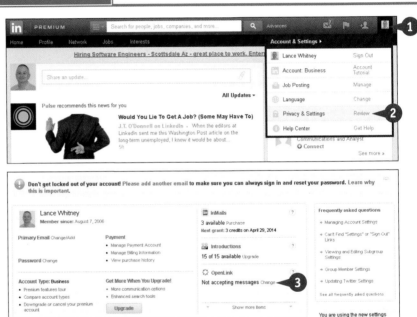

LinkedIn displays the Premium badge settings.

4 Click the **None** button (○ changes to ◉) if you do not want to display the Premium account badge on your profile; otherwise, leave the setting at Premium account.

Note: You should keep the Premium badge display enabled so other LinkedIn members can easily tell that you are a premium subscriber.

5 Click the check box (☐ changes to ☑) for **Include me in the OpenLink Network** if you want other OpenLink members to be able to send you InMail messages.

Note: The OpenLink icon will then appear on your profile and next to your name in search results.

6 Click the **Save changes** button.

7 Notice that LinkedIn changes your OpenLink status to indicate that you are accepting messages.

8 To connect with any OpenLink member, open the person's profile.

Note: The profile displays the OpenLink icon if the person is receptive to receiving messages through OpenLink.

9 Click the **send [name of person] InMail** button.

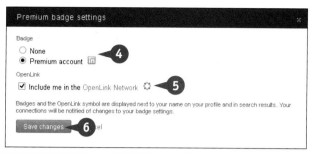

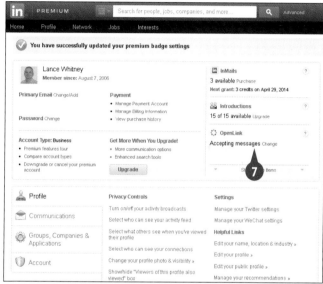

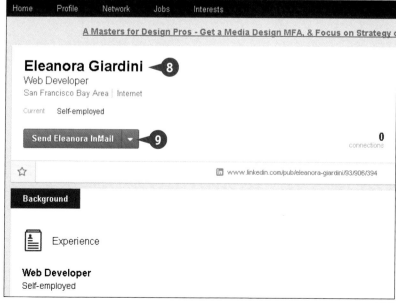

continued ▶ **199**

To connect with someone using OpenLink, you compose a message with your contact details and an explanation as to why you are contacting that person.

Use OpenLink to Connect with Members (continued)

⑩ Keep the check box (☑) to include your contact information checked if you want the person to see your contact details.

⑪ Type your phone number in the **Phone** field if you want to include it.

⑫ Click the **Category** field and select the option that best matches your reason for connecting with this person.

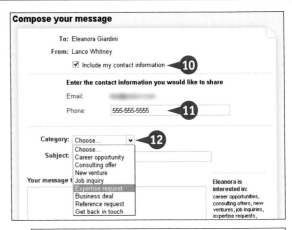

⑬ Type the subject of your message in the **Subject** field.

⑭ Type your message in the message field.

⑮ Click **Send** to send your message.

LinkedIn sends your OpenLink message.

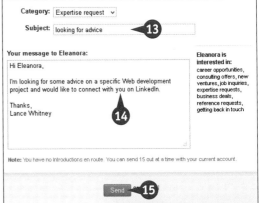

⑯ To control the types of OpenLink messages you can receive, hover over your profile photo from any LinkedIn page, and click the **Review** setting for Privacy & Settings.

Type your password at the LinkedIn Sign In page, and click **Sign In.**

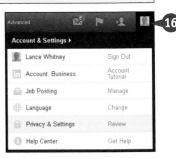

17 At the Privacy & Settings page, click the **Communications** tab.

18 In the Communications section, click the link to **Select the types of messages you're willing to receive.**

19 In the Types of messages you're willing to receive window, click one of the three buttons (◯ changes to ◉) in the Messages section: **Introductions, InMail, and OpenLink messages; Introductions and InMail only;** or **Introductions only.**

20 In the Opportunities section, click the check boxes (☐ changes to ☑) for all the opportunities you want to receive via introductions, InMail, and OpenLink.

21 Click the **Save changes** button.

LinkedIn updates your settings.

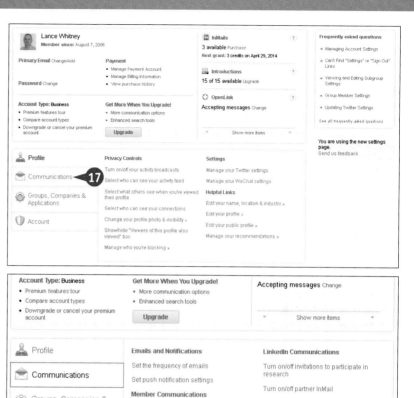

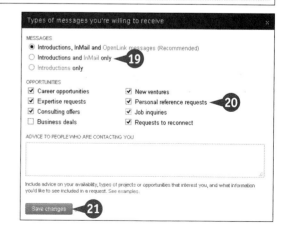

Am I restricted in how many OpenLink messages I can send?
No, with a premium subscription, you can send an unlimited number of OpenLink messages.

Cancel Your Premium Plan

Linked In's premium plans offer a variety of benefits, but they come at a cost. And at some point, you may feel the cost is too great to justify whatever benefits you get out of the plan. Can you cancel it? Of course. You can downgrade your premium account to a more basic and less expensive plan or cancel your current plan altogether to revert back to a free plan.

Cancel Your Premium Plan

1 From any LinkedIn page, hover over your profile photo, open Accounts & Settings, and click the **Review** setting for Privacy & Settings.

2 In the Account Type section at the Privacy & Settings page, click the link to **Downgrade or cancel your premium account.**

3 Click the **Downgrade Account** button.

LinkedIn displays the payment information form for a less expensive plan.

Note: LinkedIn will apply any credit from your current account to the new account.

4 Follow steps **6** through **10** in the "Sign Up for a Premium Plan" section if you want to downgrade to this plan.

5 Otherwise, return to the Downgrade Your Premium Account page by pressing your browser's back button, and click the link to **Cancel Your Premium Account.**

LinkedIn lists the features that you will lose if you cancel your premium account.

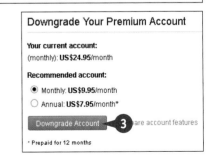

6 Click the **Continue Cancellation** button to proceed.

LinkedIn displays another page listing some of the features of your premium account.

Click the **Continue Cancellation** button on this page.

LinkedIn asks why you are cancelling your premium account.

7 Click the button (◯ changes to ◉) that best matches the reason why you are cancelling the account.

8 If necessary, type a comment in the field for **How could we have improved your Premium Account experience?**

9 Click the **Submit Cancellation** button.

LinkedIn cancels your premium account and asks you to rate it.

10 Click one of the buttons (◯ changes to ◉) that best matches your experience with your premium account, and then click the **Submit Feedback** button.

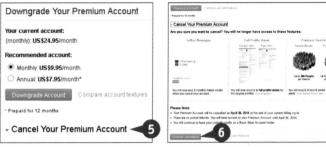

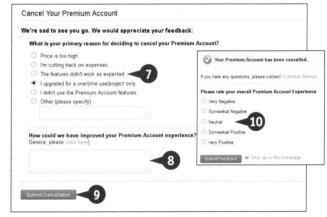

TIPS

Am I charged for a full month even after I cancel?

Yes, LinkedIn charges you until the end of the current billing cycle. Even if you cancel after one day of premium service, you are charged for a full month.

Is my premium account cancelled or downgraded immediately?

No, your premium account remains active until the end of the current billing cycle.

Do I lose my access to LinkedIn if I cancel my premium account?

No, LinkedIn simply changes your premium account back to a basic free account.

Using LinkedIn for Jobs and Business

LinkedIn can serve a role in helping you find your next job or business opportunity. Whether you are simply researching the business market or looking for a new job or career, LinkedIn's search tools and other features can point you in the right direction. Those of you who want to promote your own companies can also use LinkedIn to attract prospective clients, customers, and employees.

Find and Follow Companies

One way to learn about potential employers and other companies that interest you is to follow them on LinkedIn. By following a company, you can view its latest LinkedIn updates and discussions at your LinkedIn home page. You may also want to follow your own employer's LinkedIn page to stay current on its latest activities.

Find and Follow Companies

1 From any LinkedIn page, click the down arrow to the left of the search field and click the setting for **Companies.**

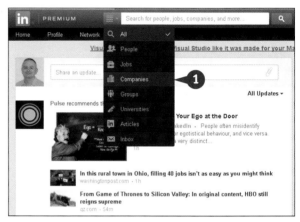

2 Type the name of a company that interests you.

LinkedIn displays search results that match the name of the company.

3 Click the name that best matches your search.

LinkedIn displays the page for that company.

④ Scroll down the page to view the company's latest LinkedIn updates.

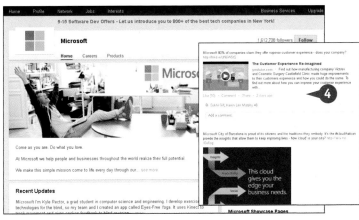

⑤ Scroll to the top of the page, and click the link for **Careers** if that category exists.

LinkedIn displays the company's Careers page.

⑥ Scroll down the page to learn about the company's career opportunities.

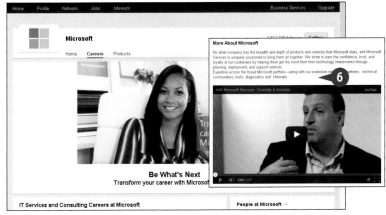

⑦ Scroll to the top of the page, and click the link for **Products** or **Services** if either of those categories exists.

LinkedIn displays a page that describes the company's products or services.

continued ▶

A s you browse through a company's LinkedIn page, you can typically learn about its careers, products, and services.

Find and Follow Companies (continued)

8 Scroll down the page to learn more.

9 Scroll to the top of the page.

10 Click the **Follow** button to follow the company.

LinkedIn adds the company to your list of followed companies.

Note: Any updates from that company will now appear among the other updates on your LinkedIn home page.

11 Click the **Home** link.

LinkedIn takes you back to the home page for the company, where you should see a section called How You're Connected. This section can help you connect with people who are affiliated with the company.

12 Click the **See all** link.

LinkedIn displays the names of members who have listed that company in their profiles.

13 Scroll down the page until you find a 1st-degree connection that you know and would like to contact for information about the company.

14 Click the **Message** button for that person's listing. Follow the steps in the "E-mail a Connection" section in Chapter 5 to send a message to that person.

15 From any LinkedIn page, click the down arrow to the left of the search field and click the setting for **Companies.**

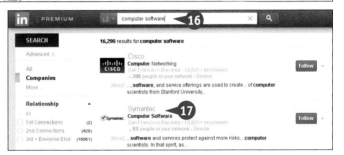

16 Type the name of an industry or profession that interests you, and click the search icon.

LinkedIn displays a list of companies that match your search term.

17 Click the link for a company that interests you.

18 Repeat steps **4** to **10** to learn more about that company and follow it.

TIP

Why do I not see a Careers page for a certain company?
Not all companies have a Careers page, but you should find one at most large employers.

View Companies that You Follow

You can view all the LinkedIn updates from companies you follow at your home page. But you can also find the updates and other details about them through a dedicated Companies page. LinkedIn's Companies page lists all of the firms that you follow so you can view a specific company, read and respond to its updates, and unfollow it if it no longer interests you.

View Companies that You Follow

1 From any LinkedIn page, hover over the **Interests** menu and click the link for **Companies.**

LinkedIn displays the latest updates from the companies you follow.

2 Scroll down the page to see all the updates.

3 Click an update that interests you to read the full story.

LinkedIn opens the story in a new browser tab or window.

Close the window to return to the Companies page.

4 Scroll to the top of the Companies page, and click the link for **Following.**

LinkedIn displays a list of all companies that you are following.

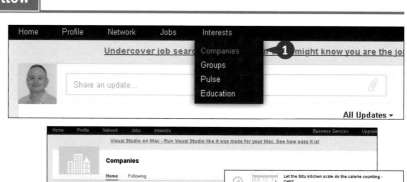

5 Click the name of a specific company to view its page.

LinkedIn displays the page for that company.

Click the back button in your browser to return to Companies page.

LinkedIn displays the full list of companies you follow.

6 To unfollow a company, hover your mouse over the link that reads **Following.**

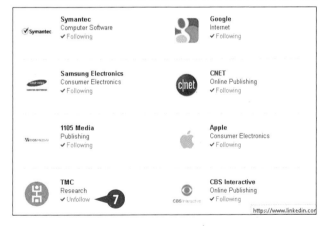

The link changes to read **Unfollow.**

7 Click the link to unfollow that company.

Click your browser's Reload or Refresh button to refresh the page.

The company you unfollowed no longer appears on the page.

TIP

How many companies can I follow?
You can follow as many companies as you want but remember that all of their updates will appear on your LinkedIn Home page.

Search for Jobs

Linkedin's primary purpose is to help you connect with other professionals. But the site can also help you connect with specific jobs. LinkedIn offers a Jobs page where you can search for positions based on industry, location, and other attributes. You can also save your job searches and opt to receive e-mail updates from LinkedIn when new jobs that match your parameters arise.

Search for Jobs

1 From any LinkedIn page, click the **Jobs** menu.

LinkedIn displays its Jobs page to show open positions based on the location you listed in your profile.

2 Start typing another location in the location box if you want to expand the search geographically.

Note: You should start by typing the name of a state.

LinkedIn displays a list of locations that match the one you typed.

3 Click the location you want to add.

LinkedIn updates the jobs list to expand to the new location.

4 Add another location if you want.

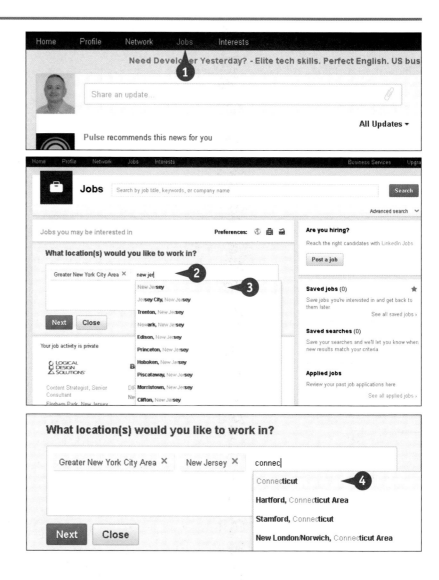

212

5 Remove a location by clicking the **X** (⊠) in its button.

6 Click **Next.**

LinkedIn asks you to specify the preferred size of a potential employer based on the number of employees.

7 Move the left lever to the right to increase the minimum number of employees.

What location(s) would you like to work in?

Greater New York City Area ✕   New Jersey ✕   Connecticut ✕ **5**

Enter a location

6

Next   Close

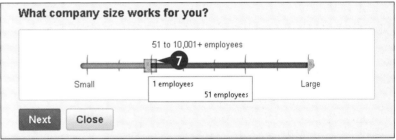

What company size works for you?

51 to 10,001+ employees

7

Small   1 employees   Large
        51 employees

Next   Close

8 Move the right lever to the left to decrease the maximum number of employees.

LinkedIn updates the list of jobs.

9 Click **Next.**

LinkedIn asks you which industries interest you.

10 Check the boxes (☐ changes to ☑) of any industries that match your career interests.

LinkedIn again updates the list of jobs.

11 Click **Finish.**

LinkedIn saves your preferences to apply to any future job searches you conduct on the site.

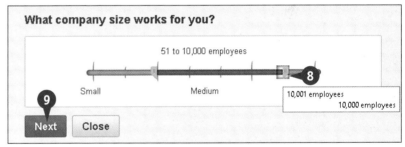

What company size works for you?

51 to 10,000 employees

8

Small   Medium   10,001 employees
                  10,000 employees

9

Next   Close

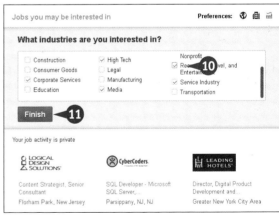

Jobs you may be interested in   Preferences: 🌐 🗄 📊

What industries are you interested in?

☐ Construction   ☑ High Tech   Nonprofit
☐ Consumer Goods   ☐ Legal   ☑ Re... **10** ...vel, and
☑ Corporate Services ☐ Manufacturing   Entertai...
☐ Education   ☑ Media   ☑ Service Industry
                                         ☐ Transportation

Finish **11**

Your job activity is private

LOGICAL DESIGN SOLUTIONS   CyberCoders   LEADING HOTELS

Content Strategist, Senior   SQL Developer - Microsoft   Director, Digital Product
Consultant   SQL Server,...   Development and...
Florham Park, New Jersey   Parsippany, NJ, NJ   Greater New York City Area

continued ▶

After you set all of the preferences for your job search, you can modify any of them individually.

Search for Jobs (continued)

12 To modify a preference, click its icon.

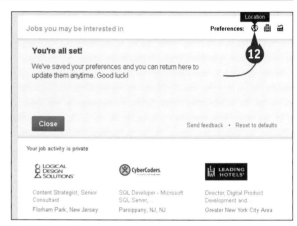

13 Change the settings for that preference.

14 Click **Next** to get to the next preference.

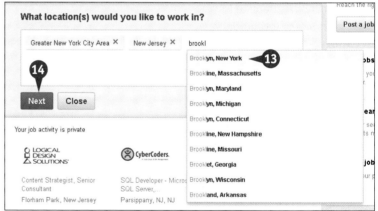

15 If necessary, change the settings for that preference and click **Next.**

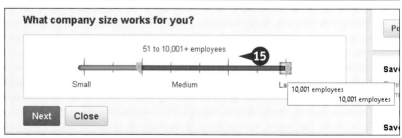

16 Change the settings for the third preference, and click **Finish** to complete your changes.

17 Click the link to **Reset to defaults** if you want to revert all your preferences back to their initial settings.

LinkedIn asks if you are sure you want to reset your "Jobs you may be interested in" preferences to their default values.

Note: Resetting your preferences back to their defaults loses all of your customizations.

18 Click **Reset** if you want to set the preferences back to their defaults. If not, skip to step **20**.

19 Follow steps **2** to **11** to set up your preferences again.

continued ▶

After you are satisifed with all of the settings for your preferences, you can scroll through the list of job results.

Search for Jobs (continued)

20 At the end of the process, click **Close** to close the preferences window.

LinkedIn updates the list of jobs based on your preferences.

Note: You can always change the settings for any preference by clicking its icon.

21 Scroll down the list to view the suggested jobs.

Note: By default, LinkedIn looks for openings based on the job titles and positions you listed in your profile.

22 Scroll back to the top of your page.

23 To narrow your job search by position, type a specific job title or profession in the Search field at the top of the page.

24 Click the **Advanced search** link (▾).

LinkedIn displays an Advanced search form where you can specify the country, ZIP Code, industry, and job function.

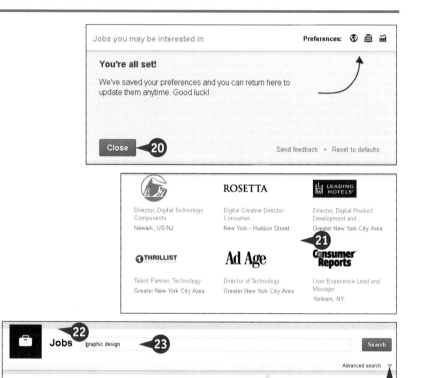

25 Confirm the country in the **Country** field.

26 Confirm the current ZIP Code, or type a specific ZIP Code in the **Zip code** field.

27 Check the boxes (☐ changes to ☑) for all the industries to include in your job search.

28 Check the boxes (☐ changes to ☑) for all the job functions to include in your search.

29 Click the **Search** button.

Note: The salary option is available only to people who have a Job Seeker Premium account.

LinkedIn runs a job search based on your parameters.

30 To save your current search, click the **Save search** link at the top of the page.

LinkedIn displays a Saved Searches form through which you can save your current search parameters.

31 Type a name for your search in the **Title** field.

LinkedIn can also e-mail you new results that match your search on a regular basis.

32 Click the **Alert** field, and click the appropriate option to set the frequency of the e-mails: **Never, Daily, Weekly,** or **Monthly.**

33 Click the check mark (☑) to save the search.

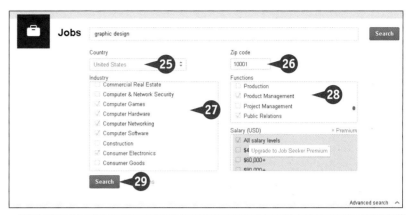

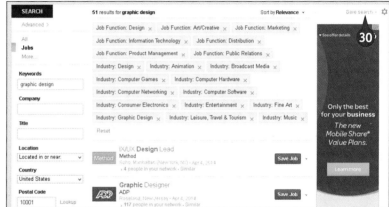

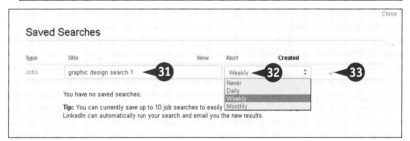

TIP

Can I narrow my job search still further?
Yes, you can further narrow your search through the search fields on the left by typing a specific company name or job title, and/or by adjusting the location.

View and Apply for Jobs that Interest You

After you find companies and jobs that spark your interest, as described in the preceding three sections, you can view and save those jobs so you can easily keep track of them. You can also apply to a job either through a link to the employer's own website or directly through LinkedIn.

View and Apply for Jobs that Interest You

1 From any LinkedIn page, click the **Interests** menu and then click the **Companies** link.

2 On the Companies page, click the link for **Following.**

3 Click the name of a company whose jobs you want to view, and on the company's LinkedIn page, click the **Careers** menu.

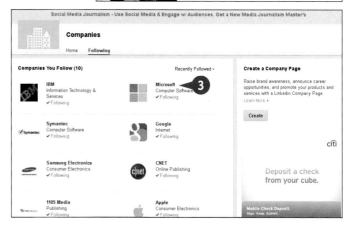

④ Scroll down the company's careers page, and click the link to see more jobs.

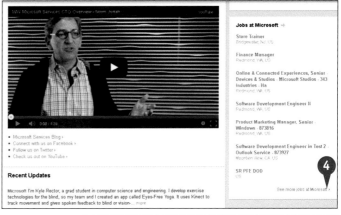

⑤ Scroll down the jobs page, and click a job that interests you.

LinkedIn displays a page with a detailed description of that job.

⑥ Click **Save** if you want to save that job.

⑦ Click your browser's back button to return to the list of jobs.

Repeat steps **6** and **7** for any other jobs that interest you both at the current company and at any other companies you follow.

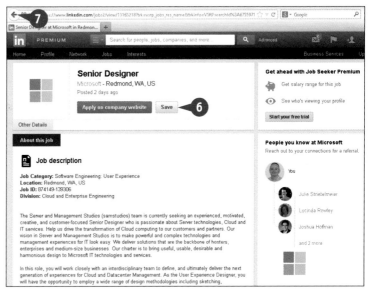

continued ▶

You can save jobs that interest you and then view all of them together before applying to specific ones.

View and Apply for Jobs that Interest You (continued)

⑧ Click the **Jobs** menu at the top of the page.

⑨ Assuming that you have saved one or more job searches as described in the previous task, click the name of a search you want to use.

LinkedIn displays the latest results for that search.

⑩ Click a job that interests you.

LinkedIn displays a page with a detailed description of that job.

⑪ Click **Save** to save that job.

Click your browser's back button to return to the list of jobs.

Repeat steps **10** and **11** for any other jobs that interest you.

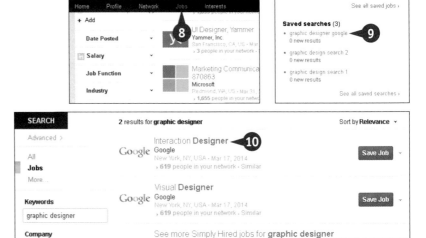

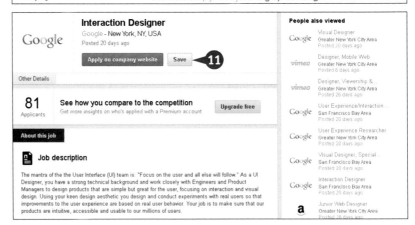

12 To view all your saved jobs, click the **Jobs** menu at the top of the page.

LinkedIn returns you to the Jobs page.

13 In the Saved Jobs section, click the link to **See all saved jobs.**

LinkedIn displays a list of all your saved jobs.

14 Click the link for a job for which you want to apply.

LinkedIn displays the job description page. For most jobs, the page displays a button at the top that says Apply on company website.

15 Click the **Apply on company website** button.

LinkedIn opens a separate browser tab or window to that company's website, through which you can apply for that job.

When you are finished, close the page for the company's website to return to the job description.

Click your browser's back button to return to your Saved jobs page.

16 Click the link for another job for which you want to apply.

LinkedIn displays the job description page. For some jobs, the page displays an Apply now button, through which you can apply for the job directly from LinkedIn.

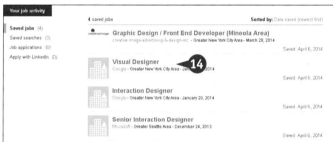

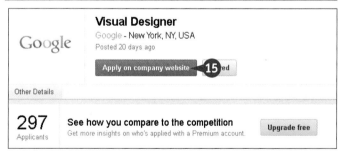

continued ▶

Y ou apply for most jobs through the employer's website, but you can apply for some jobs directly through LinkedIn.

View and Apply for Jobs that Interest You (continued)

17 Click the **Apply now** button.

LinkedIn displays an Apply with your profile window.

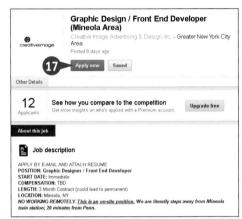

18 Type your phone number in the **Phone number** field.

19 Click the **Upload a File** link if you want to upload your resume or a cover letter.

20 Click the **Browse** button.

21 In the File Upload window, double-click the resume or cover letter you want to upload.

Note: Your resume or cover letter must be a Microsoft Word document or Adobe PDF file no larger than 5MB in size.

22 Click the **Submit** button to apply for the job.

23 To view jobs for which you have applied, click the **Jobs** menu at the top of the page.

24 On the Jobs page, click the link to **See all applied jobs.**

TIPS

Can anyone else see that I am looking for jobs on LinkedIn?

Your actual job search and applications remain private. LinkedIn does not send out any updates when you view or apply for a job.

How do I keep my current employer from finding out that I am looking for jobs on LinkedIn?

One option is to turn off activity broadcasts that normally send out updates whenever you change your profile or add new connections. That process is described in the Turn Your Activity Broadcasts On or Off section of Chapter 12.

What else can I do on LinkedIn to increase my chances of landing the right job?

On the Jobs page, LinkedIn displays a Premium Job Search Tip with useful advice that you can follow.

Does LinkedIn offer any other help or advice on conducting a job search?

You can check out LinkedIn's list of Frequently Asked Questions for more tips on job searches at http://premium.linkedin.com/jobsearch/faq.html.

Does LinkedIn offer other options to help with job searches?

Yes, you can always try LinkedIn's Premium Job Seeker plan, even just for a month, to see if you find it of value. This plan offers added benefits beyond those available through a free basic account. The Job Seeker plan and other premium accounts are described in Chapter 9.

Follow News and Influencers

One way to stay in touch with the business world on LinkedIn is to follow the site's news stories. A LinkedIn feature called Pulse offers news stories based on specific categories, such as accounting, finance, and technology. LinkedIn also provides a publishing forum for business leaders and other *influencers* through which they can write stories and columns of interest and value to LinkedIn members.

Follow News and Influencers

1 From any LinkedIn page, click the **Interests** menu and then click the **Pulse** link.

LinkedIn displays a page inviting you to follow influencers and channels. You can click the tabs at the top of the page to manually explore your choices or ask for LinkedIn's Help to get started.

Note: This page appears only if you have not yet set up any channels or influencers on Pulse.

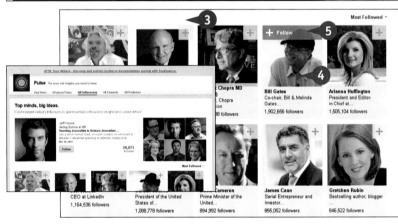

2 Click the **All Influencers** link at the top of the page to manually choose the influencers you want to follow.

LinkedIn displays the All Influencers screen for you to select the people you want to follow.

3 Scroll down the page until you see an influencer you want to follow.

4 Hover your mouse over the person's photo.

As you hover over the photo, the plus symbol displays the word **Follow.**

⑤ Click the **Follow** button to follow that person.

Scroll down through the rest of the page, and repeat steps **4** and **5** for other influencers you want to follow.

⑥ To view an influencer's posts to help you decide if you want to follow that person, click any part of the photo below the **Follow** button.

LinkedIn displays a list of posts by that person.

⑦ Click a particular post to read it.

LinkedIn displays the post.

Click your browser's back button to return to the lists of posts, and click it again to return to the list of all influencers.

⑧ Click the **Follow** button if you want to follow the person whose posts you just read.

⑨ Scroll to the top of the page, and click the **All Channels** link.

LinkedIn displays the All Channels page for you to select the channels you want to follow.

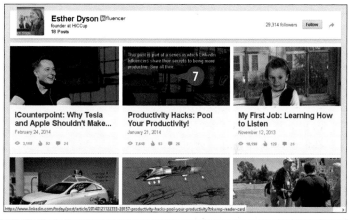

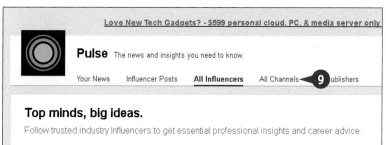

continued ▶

You can find stories and columns through channels that focus on specific topics of interest.

Follow News and Influencers (continued)

10 Scroll down the page to view the list of channels.

11 Hover over any unchecked channel that interests you.

As you hover over an unchecked channel, a **Follow** option appears.

12 Click the **Follow** option to follow that particular channel.

13 Follow any other channels that interest you.

14 Scroll to the top of the page, and click the **All Publishers** link.

LinkedIn displays the All Publishers page for you to select the publishers you want to follow.

15 Scroll down the page, hover over a publisher you want to follow, and click the **Follow** button.

Select any other publishers you want to follow.

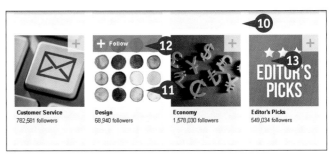

Customer Service
782,581 followers

Design
68,940 followers

Economy
1,578,030 followers

Editor's Picks
549,034 followers

Visual Studio on OSX - --Simultaneously run Xcode on Mac and Visual Studio on W

Pulse The news and insights you need to know.

Your News   Influencer Posts   All Influencers   All Channels   **All Publishers**

Timely information, delivered to you.

The Economist
150,874 followers

Variety
16,351 followers

Mashable
181,179 followers

Associated Press
27,018 followers

16 Scroll to the top of the page, and click the **Your News** link.

LinkedIn displays stories and posts from all the influencers, channels, and publishers you follow.

17 Click a specific story or post that you want to read.

LinkedIn displays that item.

Click your browser's back button to return to the Your News section.

18 Click the **All Influencers** link at the top of the page.

19 On the all Influencers page, hover over the **Most Followed** link on the right.

20 Click the link for **Following.**

LinkedIn displays a list of all the influencers you follow.

21 Hover over the photo of an influencer you no longer want to follow, and click the **Unfollow** button.

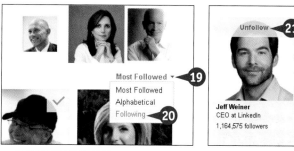

22 Scroll to the top of the page, and click the **All Channels** link.

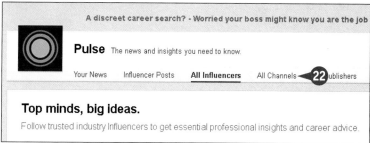

23 Scroll down the list, hover over any channel you no longer want to follow, and click the **Unfollow** button.

24 Repeat the same step for the All Publishers page for any publishers you no longer want to follow.

Post a Job

Employers can use LinkedIn to post jobs and reach out to prospective candidates. Naturally, you have to pay a fee to post a job on LinkedIn. But you may find it an effective way of attracting the right talent. And you can learn a great deal about a job applicant directly through that person's LinkedIn profile.

Post a Job

1 From any LinkedIn page, click the **Jobs** menu at the top of the page.

2 On the Jobs page, click the **Post a job** button.

LinkedIn displays a page with information and advice about posting a job.

3 In the Learn more section, click the link to **Write the perfect post.**

LinkedIn displays a window with tips on creating job posts.

4 Scroll down the window to read all the information.

5 Click the right arrow at the bottom of the window to view the next screen with information on posting jobs.

Continue scrolling and then clicking the right arrow to read all the job posting tips offered by LinkedIn.

6 Click the **X** to close the window.

7 Click the **Post a Job** button.

LinkedIn displays a form for you to complete to post your job.

8 Start typing the name of your company in the **Company** field, and select the name if it appears in LinkedIn's list of suggestions. Otherwise, finish typing the name.

9 Type a description of your company in the **Company Description** field.

Note: LinkedIn may have already filled in the company name and description field based on your current employer.

10 Click the **Industry** field, and select your company's industry from LinkedIn's list.

11 Click the plus icon to add another industry if necessary, and repeat step **10**.

Complete the fields for **Job Title, Experience, Job Function, Employment Type,** and **Job Description.**

12 Type the skills and expertise needed in the **Desired Skills and Expertise** field.

13 Check the box (□ changes to ☑) for **Veteran Commitment** if you want to make it easier for veterans to find this job.

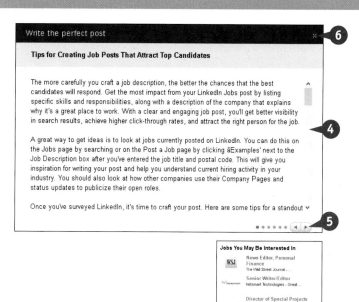

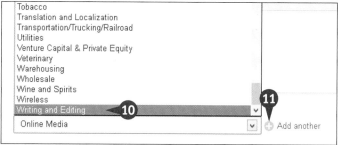

continued ▶

Post a Job (continued)

14 In the How candidates apply section, keep the button (⦿) selected to **Collect applications on LinkedIn and be notified by e-mail** if you want to receive notices by e-mail.

15 Type or confirm the e-mail address that you want to use to receive applications.

16 Otherwise, click the button (◯ changes to ⦿) for **Direct applicants to an external site to apply** if the job is posted on your own company's website and you want to direct applicants to your site.

17 Keep the check mark (☑) under **Job Poster** checked if you want to show your own profile summary on the listing for this job.

18 In the **Country** field, confirm the country in which the job is located.

19 In the **Postal Code** field, type the ZIP Code in which the job is located.

20 Leave the button (⦿) for the **30-day posting** active if you have fewer than five jobs.

21 Otherwise, click the button (◯ changes to ⦿) for one of the other two options (**5-job pack** or **10-job pack**) if you have five or ten jobs to post and want to save money on each post.

22 Click the **Preview** button if you want to preview your job post before posting it live.

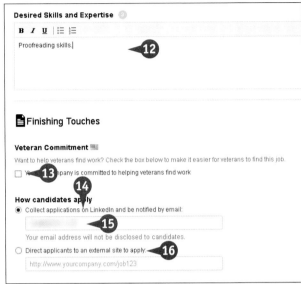

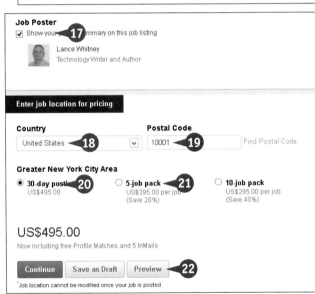

23 Click the **X** (☒) to close the Preview window.

24 Click **Continue** to move to the next screen.

LinkedIn displays a page to Showcase your job to the right candidates.

25 Check the box for (☐ changes to ☑) **Yes, sponsor my job** if you want to pay a fee for LinkedIn to promote your job post through a sponsored placement.

LinkedIn suggests an amount that you would pay each time someone clicks your sponsored job post.

26 In the **Cost per click** field, type a different amount if you want to change it.

27 In the **Total budget** field, type the total amount of money you are willing to pay for your job post sponsorship.

28 Click **Continue.**

LinkedIn displays a payment information form for you to enter your credit card and billing details.

29 Confirm your name and type your credit card information in the **Credit or Debit Card Information** section.

30 Review or type your name, location, and phone number in the **Billing Information** section.

Click the **Review order** button, and follow the subsequent screens to review and place your order.

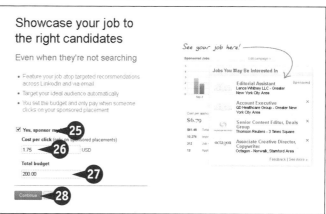

Build a Company Page

To fully promote your business, you may want to create a company page. Through such a page, you can publicize your organization, market your products and services, and advertise job openings. You can also post updates about your business to share the latest news and spark conversations among people who follow your page.

Build a Company Page

1 From any LinkedIn page, click the **Interests** menu at the top of the page and then click **Companies.**

2 On the Companies page, click the **Learn More** link.

LinkedIn displays frequently asked questions for company pages.

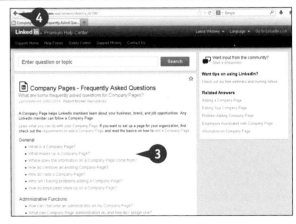

3 Click the links on the page to view information and advice on company pages.

4 Click your browser's back button to return to the LinkedIn Companies page.

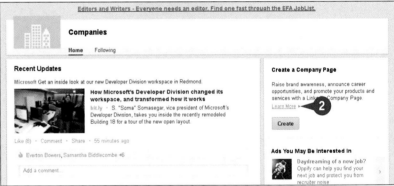

5 On the Companies page, click the **Create** button.

6 On the Add a Company page, type the name of your company in the **Company name** field.

7 Type your company e-mail address in the field for **Your e-mail address at company.**

8 Check the box (☐ changes to ☑) to verify that you are the official representative of this company and can act on its behalf to create the page.

9 Click **Continue.**

LinkedIn sends a confirmation e-mail to the e-mail address you listed.

10 Open the e-mail account you listed on the form, and select the confirmation mail from LinkedIn.

11 Click the **Click here** link to confirm your e-mail address.

After the confirmation process is complete, LinkedIn displays a form that you complete to create your company page.

12 Confirm your company name in the **Company Name** field.

13 Type a description of the company in the **Company Description** field.

Note: Your description must be at least 250 characters in length.

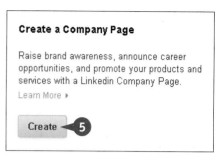

Create a Company Page

Raise brand awareness, announce career opportunities, and promote your products and services with a LinkedIn Company Page.

Learn More ▸

Create **5**

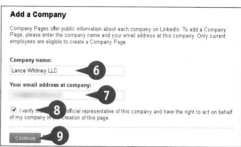

Add a Company

Company Pages offer public information about each company on LinkedIn. To add a Company Page, please enter the company name and your email address at this company. Only current employees are eligible to create a Company Page.

Company name:
Lance Whitney LLC **6**

Your email address at company:
7

☑ I verify that I am the official representative of this company and have the right to act on behalf of my company in the creation of this page. **8**

Continue **9**

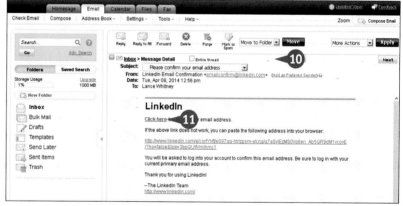

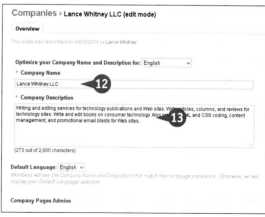

continued ▶

Build a Company Page (continued)

14 In the field for **Designated Admins,** type the names of any other people on LinkedIn who need to administer the page.

15 On the right side of the form under **Company Type,** click the option for **Public Company** and change the setting if necessary.

16 Under **Company size,** click the option for **myself only** and change the setting to describe the size of your company if necessary.

17 In the **Company Website URL** field, type the address for your company's website.

18 In the **Main Company Industry** field, click the option for **Accounting** and change the setting to apply to your company.

19 In the **Company Operating Status** field, click the option for **Operating** and change the setting to reflect your company's current status.

20 In the **Year Founded** field, type the year your company started.

21 In the **Company Location** field, click the option to **Add another location** if you need to add another physical location for your company.

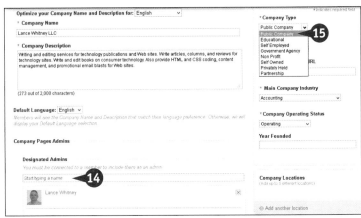

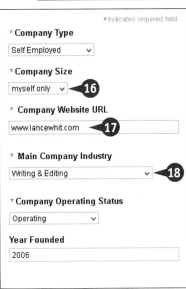

22 Click the **Add image** link below the image window to add a company logo or other suitable image.

23 In the Add image window, click the **Browse** button to browse to the image you want to upload.

In the File Upload window, double-click the file you want to use as your image.

24 In the Add image window, crop the image to conform to LinkedIn's size requirements and click **Save.**

LinkedIn displays the image on your company page.

25 Click the **Add logo** link for the Standard Logo image, and repeat steps **23** to **24** to upload a suitable image if you need one.

26 Click the **Add logo** link for the Square Logo, and repeat steps **23** to **24** to upload an image if necessary.

27 In the **Company Specialties** section, type any specialties of your company that you want to highlight.

28 When you are finished, scroll to the top of the page and click the **Publish** button.

LinkedIn publishes your company page and displays it for you.

To edit your page, hover your mouse over the down arrow next to the **Edit** button at the top.

Click **Edit page** to revise any of the information on the page.

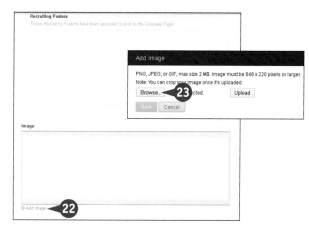

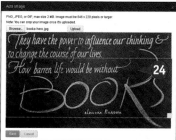

TIP

Are there any restrictions on the images that I can upload?

The images must be PNG, JPEG, or GIF files with a maximum size of 2 MB.

CHAPTER 11

Using LinkedIn for Education

LinkedIn is primarily thought of as a tool for professional career networking. But the site also serves a valuable role in the world of education. Alumni can use LinkedIn to keep track of their own universities. High-school students and people who plan to resume or continue their education can use the site to research potential schools. And colleges can market themselves through dedicated pages on LinkedIn.

Use LinkedIn as a Prospective Student

Whether you are a current student looking to move on to college or graduate school or a working professional who wants to return to school, LinkedIn can help you in your search. You can find and research schools based on your field of study, location, and other factors. You can learn about different universities throughout the world by visiting their pages, asking questions, and connecting with students and alumni.

Use LinkedIn as a Prospective Student

1 From any LinkedIn page, click the **Interests** menu and then click **Education.**

LinkedIn displays the Education page.

2 Click the link for **Prospective Students.**

LinkedIn displays the page for Prospective Students.

③ If you want to research a particular school, start typing its name in the **School Name** field.

LinkedIn displays a list of potential matches.

④ Click the name of the school you want to research.

LinkedIn displays that school's University Page.

⑤ Click the **Show more** link in the General Information section.

LinkedIn displays more details about the school, including alumni statistics, contact information, student population, and tuition costs.

⑥ Click the **Homepage** link to view the school's website.

LinkedIn opens the school's own website in a separate window.

Close the school's website when you are finished viewing it and want to return to its LinkedIn page.

⑦ If the school's e-mail address appears, click the link for it if you want to send a message.

Your default e-mail program pops up for you to write and send your message.

Note: You might e-mail the school if you want to receive brochures and other information in the mail or want to schedule an appointment to visit the campus.

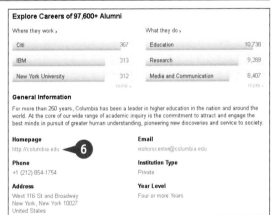

continued ▶

You can learn a lot about a school through the information and discussions on its LinkedIn page.

Use LinkedIn as a Prospective Student (continued)

8 Return to the school's LinkedIn page, and scroll down the page to view the various updates and discussions.

9 Follow the steps in the "Respond to an Update" section in Chapter 4 to like, share, or comment on an update.

10 Follow the steps in the "Post Your Own Updates" section in Chapter 4 if you want to ask a question or post your own comment about the school.

Note: Posting questions can be a good way to learn about the school because it can elicit responses from current students, alumni, and other people connected to the school.

11 Click the **Follow** button at the top of the page to follow the school.

Note: Following the school means that you will see all its updates and discussions on your LinkedIn home page.

12 Scroll to the Who you know section.

13 Click the link for **first-degree connections** if it appears.

LinkedIn displays the names of any first-degree connections who have attended the school.

14 Click the **Send a Message** button for a connection that you want to contact about the school.

15 Fill out the message form with a subject and the message itself, and click the **Send Message** button.

Click your browser's back button until you return to the school's University page.

16 Read the section at the top that tells you where alumni of the school work and what they do.

17 Click the **more** link in either the Where they work section or the What they do section.

LinkedIn displays a more detailed page showing you where alumni of the school live, where they work, and what they do.

18 Click the **Show More** link in the top section.

LinkedIn displays more locations, companies, and industries for alumni.

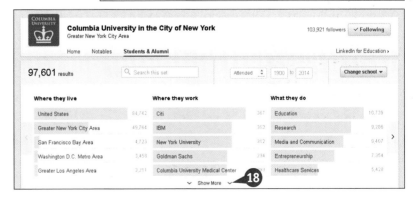

continued ▶

You can find alumni of any school through the school's University page.

Use LinkedIn as a Prospective Student (continued)

19 Click a specific location, employer, or industry to narrow the list of alumni to just that item.

Note: You can also click multiple locations, employers, and industries to then expand the alumni search.

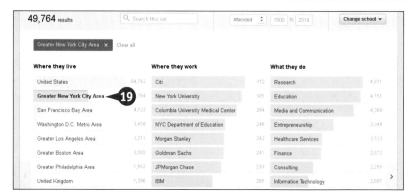

20 To remove any items from the search, scroll to the top of the page and click the **X** for the item or items you want to remove.

21 To reset your search to include all items, click the **Clear all** link at the top.

22 Scroll further down the page to see the names of alumni.

23 Click the name of an alumnus that you want to invite to your LinkedIn network, and complete and send the invitation.

Note: You can narrow the search for alumni by following the steps in the "Find Alumni" section of Chapter 3.

24 Return to the school's page, and scroll down to the section for similar schools.

LinkedIn displays a list of schools with fields of study and other attributes similar to those of the current school.

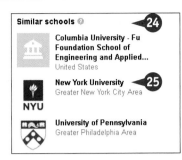

25 Click the name of a school you want to view.

26 Follow steps **5** to **23** to investigate that school and connect with alumni.

27 To further search for a range of colleges based on a field of study, click the down arrow next to the search field at the top of the page.

28 Click the option for **Universities.**

29 Type the field of study that interests you in the search field, and click the search icon.

LinkedIn displays a list of universities that offer your field of study.

Should I start my school search on LinkedIn?

No, not necessarily. As described in some of the steps in this section, you can search LinkedIn to discover schools based on a field of study and other criteria. But you will find LinkedIn of the greatest benefit if you have already started gathering a list of schools that interest you.

What are the advantages of using LinkedIn to research schools?

LinkedIn can provide information, updates, and potential connections for schools that interest you. But the site can also suggest more schools similar to ones that you are already researching.

Use LinkedIn as a Current Student

College students can use LinkedIn to follow their schools and to search the job market. Your university's LinkedIn page will keep you up to date on the latest activities, updates, and other information about your school. And employers who use LinkedIn can lead you to entry-level jobs and internships to help you kick off your career.

Use LinkedIn as a Current Student

1 From any LinkedIn page, click the **Interests** menu and then click **Education.**

LinkedIn displays the Education page.

2 Click the link for **Students.**

LinkedIn displays the Students page with three suggested steps to help you.

3 In the Step 1 section, start typing the name of your current school in the **School Name** field.

LinkedIn displays a list of potential matches.

4 Click the name of your school from LinkedIn's list.

LinkedIn displays that school's University page.

5 Click the **Show more** link under General Information to see more details about the school.

LinkedIn displays alumni statistics, contact details, and other information.

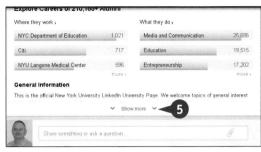

6 Scroll down the page to view updates and discussions about the school.

Follow the steps in the "Respond to an Update" section in Chapter 4 to like, share, or comment on an update.

Follow the steps in the "Post Your Own Updates" section in Chapter 4 if you want to ask a question or post your own comment about your school.

7 Scroll to the top of the page.

8 Click the **Follow** button to follow your school.

9 If you have not yet added your school to your profile, make sure the option in the Add to profile section says: **I'm a student here.**

10 Click the button to **Add to profile.**

LinkedIn displays an Add Education form.

11 Fill out the Add Education form, and click the **Save Changes** button to add it to your profile.

continued ▶

12 Return to the Education page, and click the link for **Students.**

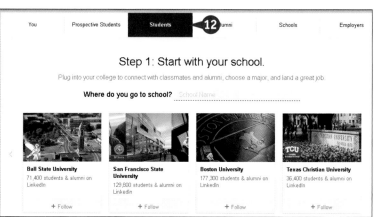

13 Scroll down to the Step 2 section.

14 If you want to beef up your LinkedIn profile even further, click the **Enhance your profile** link.

LinkedIn opens your profile in Edit mode.

15 Follow the steps in Chapters 2 and 4 to edit and enhance your profile.

16 Return to the Education page, and click the link for **Students.**

17 Scroll down to the Step 3 section.

18 Click the link to **Search Jobs.**

LinkedIn displays a page called "Jobs For Students And Recent Graduates."

19 In the Companies looking to hire section, click the **View entry-level jobs and internships** link if the company listed is of interest to you.

LinkedIn displays a list of entry-level jobs and internships.

Note: LinkedIn continually changes the company highlighted for its entry-level jobs and internships.

20 To narrow the search by location and other criteria, follow steps **35** to **38** in the "Search for Jobs" section of Chapter 10.

21 To save and apply for a specific job, follow the steps in the "View and Apply for Jobs that Interest You" section in Chapter 10.

22 Return to the "Jobs For Students And Recent Graduates" page.

23 In the Recent Opportunities section, click the **See More** link.

LinkedIn displays entry-level jobs and internships for a variety of companies.

TIP

Can I find more jobs for students and graduates?
Yes, at the "Jobs for Students and Recent Graduates" page, click the box for **Any Job Function**, click a specific job function from the list, and then click the **Search Jobs** button.

Use LinkedIn as an Alumnus

Those of you who are graduates of a university can use LinkedIn to follow your school and connect with fellow alumni. Former classmates can be a good resource if you are looking to hire someone for your business or searching for professional opportunities for yourself.

Use LinkedIn as an Alumnus

1 From any LinkedIn page, click the **Interests** menu and then click **Education.**

LinkedIn displays the Education page.

2 Click the link for **Alumni.**

LinkedIn displays the Alumni page.

3 Start typing the name of your school in the **School Name** field, and select your school from LinkedIn's list.

LinkedIn displays the school's University page.

4 Click the **Show more** link under General Information if you want to see more details about the school.

LinkedIn displays contact details and other information about your school.

5 Scroll down the page to view updates and discussions about the school.

6 Follow the steps in the "Respond to an Update" section in Chapter 4 to like, share, or comment on an update.

7 Follow the steps in the "Post Your Own Updates" section in Chapter 4 if you want to ask a question or post your own comment about your school.

8 Scroll to the top of the page.

9 Click the **Follow** button to follow your school.

10 In the Who you know section, click the link for **second-degree connections.**

LinkedIn displays the names of alumni who are 2nd-degree connections.

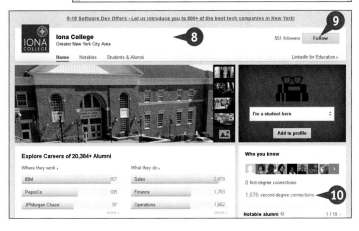

continued ▶

You can find and connect with your fellow alumni through your school's University page.

Use LinkedIn as an Alumnus (continued)

11 To narrow the results, click and change the starting and ending attendance dates at the top of the page.

12 Check the box (☐ changes to ☑) to **Include people with no dates.**

13 Click specific locations, employers, and/or industries if you want to narrow the results even further.

Note: You can click the **Show More** link in the top section to see more locations, employers, and industries.

14 Scroll down the list of results, and click the name of an alumnus you want to invite to your network.

15 Click the **Connect** button.

16 Type your message, and click the **Send Invitation** button.

Click your browser's back button until you have returned to your school's page.

17 Scroll down the page to the section on Join your alumni group.

18 Click the **Find a group** button.

LinkedIn displays a list of alumni groups for your school.

19 Click the **Join** button for any groups you want to join.

Depending on the type of group, you are either granted immediate access or told that your request to join has been received, in which case it will be evaluated.

Click your browser's back button to return to the school's page.

20 Scroll to the top of your school's page.

21 If you have not yet added your school to your profile, click the **I'm a student here** option in the Add to profile section and change that to **I'm an alumnus here.**

22 Click the **Add to profile** button.

LinkedIn displays the Add Education form.

23 Complete the Add Education form, and click the **Save Changes** button to add your school to your profile.

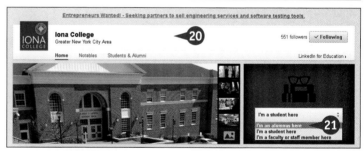

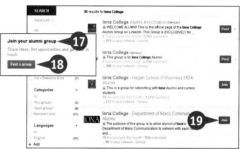

TIP

Can I view alumni from other schools?

Yes, at the page that displays connections from your own school, click the **Change School** button.

Use LinkedIn as a School Administrator

ollege administrators can use LinkedIn to promote their schools as a way of attracting and informing prospective students. Using dedicated University Pages, you can share general information about your school, post updates, and highlight prominent alumni. LinkedIn creates your initial page, but administrators at your school can then revise and enhance it.

Use LinkedIn as a School Administrator

1 From any LinkedIn page, click the **Interests** menu and then click **Education.**

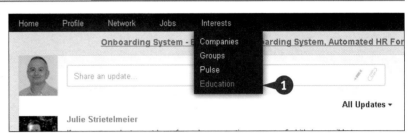

LinkedIn displays the Education page.

2 Click the link for **Schools.**

LinkedIn displays the Schools page.

3 Click the **Learn more** link to play the LinkedIn for Higher Education Video.

4 After the video is over, close the YouTube page to return to LinkedIn.

5 Back at the Schools page, click the **Learn more** link to open the Higher Education Resource Center.

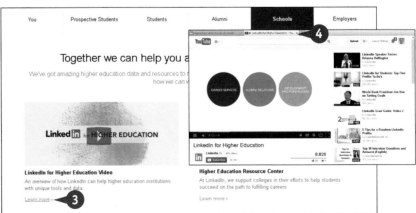

6 Scroll down the page, and click the links to view or download the various files, and other information.

7 When you are finished, click your browser's back button until you are back at the Schools page.

8 At the Schools page, start typing the name of your university in the **School Name** field and click the name from LinkedIn's list if it appears.

LinkedIn displays your school's page.

9 If you are an administrator at your school and need access to edit the page, click the setting for **I'm a student here** and change it to **I'm a faculty or staff member here.**

10 Hover your mouse over the down arrow next to **Add to profile,** and click the option to **Request admin access.**

If your school does not already have a university page, you must contact LinkedIn to request that a page be created. To send this request to LinkedIn, fill out the contact form at the following URL: http://help.linkedin.com/app/ask/path/upaq.

Higher Education Resource Center
At LinkedIn, we support colleges in their efforts to help students succeed on the path to fulfilling careers.

Learn more ›

TIP

As an administrator of my school's LinkedIn page, what information can I add or revise?
You can add and revise contact information, other details, and notable alumni. You can also post updates about your school.

Use LinkedIn as an Employer

mployers can use LinkedIn's educational pages and services to find the right talent among students. You can set up career pages to showcase opportunities for students and create ads for entry-level jobs and internships.

Use LinkedIn as an Employer

① From any LinkedIn page, click the **Interests** menu and then click **Education.**

LinkedIn displays the Education page.

② Click the link for **Employers.**

LinkedIn displays the Employer page.

③ Click the **Learn more** link in the Be the Employer of Choice section.

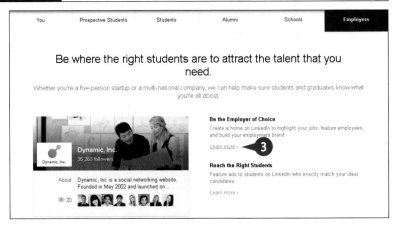

④ Notice that LinkedIn displays a page where you can learn and request a demo on how to create a career page.

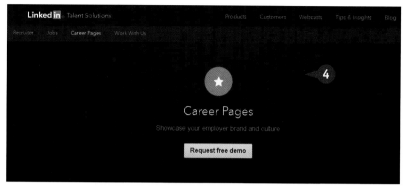

⑤ Scroll down the page, and click the various links on the page to learn more.

⑥ When you are finished, click your browser's back button to return to the Employer page.

⑦ At the Employer page, click the **Learn more** link in the Reach the Right Students section.

LinkedIn displays a Work With Us page that explains how to create custom recruitment ads.

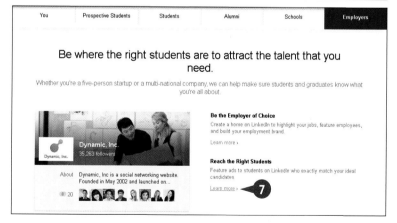

continued ▶

LinkedIn offers Career Pages and other features to help employers find the right people for entry-level jobs and internships.

Use LinkedIn as an Employer (continued)

8 Scroll down the page, and click the various links on the page to learn more.

9 When you are finished, click your browser's back button to return to the Employer page.

10 Scroll down to the section called Source Talent from Every Corner of the Globe.

11 Click the **Learn more** link for LinkedIn Recruiter.

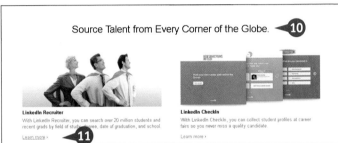

12 Notice that LinkedIn displays a page where you can learn about the site's premium Recruiter account.

13 Scroll down the page, and click the various links on the page to learn more.

14 When you are finished, click your browser's back button to return to the Employer page.

15 Click the **Learn more** link in the LinkedIn CheckIn section.

LinkedIn displays a page that explains how to use its LinkedIn CheckIn feature.

16 Scroll down the page, and click the various links on the page to learn more.

17 When you are finished, click your browser's back button to return to the Employer page.

18 Scroll to the Your jobs wanted section.

19 Click the link for **Student job portal.**

LinkedIn displays a page titled Hire the best new professionals.

20 If you want to post a free ad for a job aimed at students, click the **Post Free Jobs** button.

Follow the steps in the "Post a Job" section in Chapter 10 to post the job ad.

Source Talent from Every Corner of the Globe.

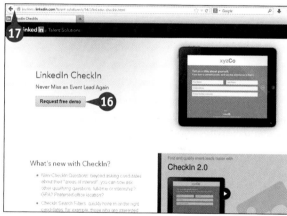

Your jobs wanted.

Post jobs for FREE on our student job portal. Thousands of students and recent grads are looking every day

Student job portal ▸

Hire the best new professionals

- Reach millions of students and recent graduates from the world's top universities
- Students are LinkedIn's fastest growing and most engaged segment
- Promote your jobs to students on LinkedIn's student jobs portal

Use LinkedIn for all your entry-level and internship hiring this year.*

Post Free Jobs

TIP

How can I learn more about the Job Recruiter accounts?
Read the section on "Review LinkedIn's Recruiter Plans" in Chapter 9.

Managing Your Profile and Account

How do you control and tweak the wide array of settings for your LinkedIn profile and account? LinkedIn offers a single Settings screen through which you can access and change a variety of options. Here you can control your security, change your password, manage your advertising preferences, and even close your account.

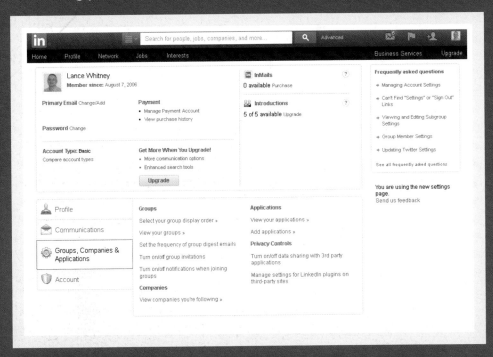

Turn Your Activity Broadcasts On or Off

You may have noticed that many of the actions you make on LinkedIn are broadcast on your *activity feed* for anyone to read. Update your profile, join a new group, follow a new company, or make a new connection, and anyone who reads your activity feed knows about it. What can you do if you do not want all your actions to be broadcast? No problem. You can easily turn them off.

Turn Your Activity Broadcasts On or Off

1 From any LinkedIn page, hover over your thumbnail LinkedIn photo in the upper-right corner.

2 From the Accounts & Settings menu, click the **Review** link for Privacy & Settings.

If required, type your password at the Sign in to LinkedIn page, and click **Sign In.**

3 At the Privacy & Settings page, click the link for **Turn on/off your activity broadcasts.**

4 In the Activity Broadcasts window, uncheck the box (☑ changes to ☐) for **Let people know when you change your profile, make recommendations, or follow companies.**

5 Click **Save Changes.**

Note: You may have a reason to turn off your activity broadcasts. As one example, you may be looking for a job and not want anyone to see your job-related activity.

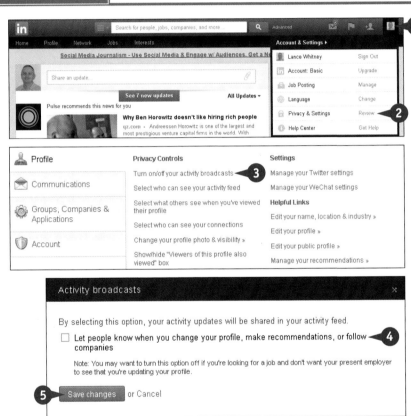

Select Who Can See Your Activity Feed

Y ou can further manage your activity feed by controlling who sees it. LinkedIn offers you four choices for who can view your feed: Everyone (all LinkedIn subscribers), Your network (your 1st-, 2nd-, and 3rd-degree connections), Your connections (only your 1st-degree connections), or Only you.

Select Who Can See Your Activity Feed

1 At the Privacy & Settings page, click the link for **Select who can see your activity feed.**

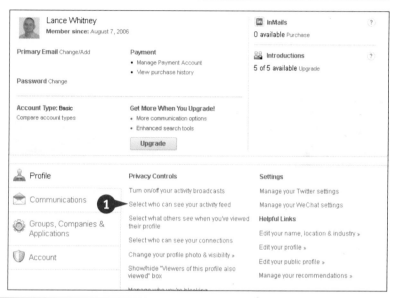

2 In the Who can see your activity feed window, click the arrow (⌄) and set the option to **Everyone, Your Network, Your Connections,** or **Only you.**

Note: You may want to open up your feed to everyone, or at least your entire network, if you want to promote something but then restrict it to only you if you are looking for a job.

3 Click **Save changes.**

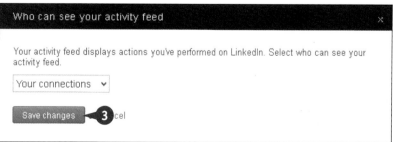

Choose How You Appear to People Whose Profile You View

When you view the profile of another LinkedIn member, that person can tell you viewed his or her profile though a page that shows viewers of that profile. By default, your profile name, title, and photo appear so the person knows who you are. But you can limit the information another LinkedIn member sees when you view that person's profile.

Choose How You Appear to People Whose Profile You View

1 At the Privacy & Settings page, click the link for **Select what others see when you've viewed their profile.**

LinkedIn displays a "What others see when you've viewed their profile" window with three options:

Your name and headline, which displays your name, title, location, and photo.

Anonymous profile characteristics, which displays your title, industry, and company.

Totally anonymous, which reveals no signs that you viewed the profile.

Note: Normally, you might want to keep your full profile info visible in case a member whose profile you view wants to connect with you. But if you are viewing profiles while looking for a job or conducting certain research, you may want to be anonymous.

2 Choose the appropriate option (◻ changes to ◉).

3 Click **Save changes.**

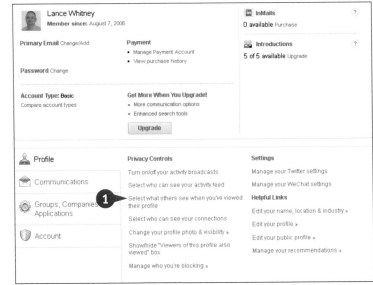

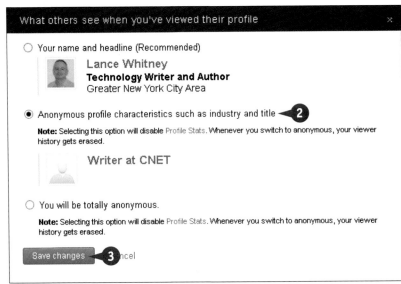

Turn Off Data Sharing with Third-Party Apps

B y default, LinkedIn can share your basic profile and contact information with third-party applications. This process ensures that your information is available to certain apps that connect to LinkedIn and that you may use. But if you would rather LinkedIn not share this information, you can easily turn off the option.

Turn Off Data Sharing with Third-Party Apps

1 At the Privacy & Settings page, click the tab for **Groups, Companies & Applications.**

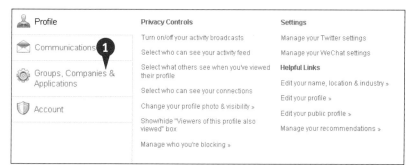

2 Click the link to **Turn on/off data sharing with 3rd party applications.**

3 At the Data sharing with third-party applications window, uncheck the box for **Yes, share my data (including base profile and contact information) with third-party applications** (☑ changes to ☐) if you want to disable that option.

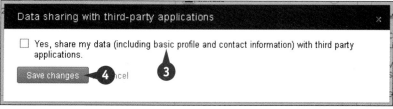

4 Click **Save Changes.**

5 Notice that LinkedIn flashes a message that you have successfully changed your data sharing setting.

Manage LinkedIn Plugins on Third-Party Sites

LinkedIn maintains a Share button and certain other plugins that you will likely see on third-party websites. Each time you use one of those buttons or plugins, LinkedIn receives information to confirm that you visited the page. But if you prefer to disable that capability for your account, you can certainly do so.

Manage LinkedIn Plugins on Third-Party Sites

1 At the Privacy & Settings page, click the tab for **Groups, Companies & Applications** if it is not already active.

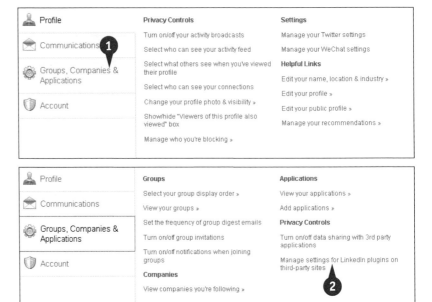

2 Click the link to **Manage settings for LinkedIn plugins on third-party sites.**

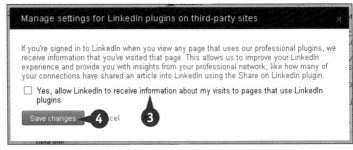

3 At the Manage settings for LinkedIn plugins on third-party sites window, uncheck the box (☑ changes to ☐) to **Yes, allow LinkedIn to receive information about my visits to pages that use LinkedIn plugins** if you want to disable that option.

4 Click **Save Changes.**

5 Notice that LinkedIn flashes a message that you have successfully changed your offsite privacy management settings.

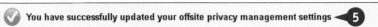

Manage Your Advertising Preferences

L ike most websites, LinkedIn makes money through advertising, specifically by displaying ads to its members. A section on the right side of your Home page entitled Ads You May Be Interested In features ads that LinkedIn hopes may appeal to you. You can learn more about how LinkedIn uses ads and also limit the types of ads you see by viewing and managing your advertising preferences.

Manage Advertising Preferences

1 At the Privacy & Settings page, click the **Account** tab.

2 Click the link to **Manage Advertising Preferences.**

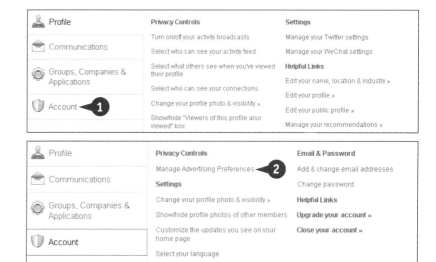

3 In the Manage Advertising Preferences window, click the **Read more** link for each of the three advertising sections: Ads by LinkedIn - Overview, Ad selection, and Protecting your personal information. Make sure to read the information provided to understand how ads work on LinkedIn.

4 Uncheck the boxes (☑ changes to ☐) for **LinkedIn may show me ads on third-party websites** and **LinkedIn may show me ads based on third-party data** if you would rather limit the types of ads LinkedIn shows you.

5 Click **Save changes.**

Show or Hide Profile Photos of Other Members

Just as you can prevent other people from seeing your profile photo, you can turn off the display of the photos of other members if you do not want to see them. LinkedIn gives you the choice of hiding photos for everyone, your extended network, your own connections, or no one.

Show or Hide Profile Photos of Other Members

1 At the Privacy & Settings page, make sure the **Account** tab is active.

2 Click the link to **Show/Hide Profile Photos of Other Members.**

3 In the Profile photos of other members window, click the arrow (⌄) to select the photos you would like to see.

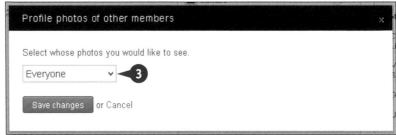

4 Click one of the four selections: **Everyone, Your network, Your connections,** or **No One.**

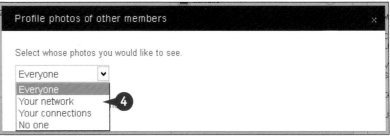

5 Click **Save changes.**

Customize the Updates You See on Your Home Page

Inundated with too many different types of updates on your LinkedIn home page? You can change your account settings to see only specific types of updates and just a certain number. For example, you can elect to see updates from your connections and job opportunities but not trending news or profile changes from the people in your network.

Customize the Updates You See on Your Home Page

1 At the Privacy & Settings page, make sure the **Account** tab is active.

2 Click the link to **Customize the Updates You See on Your Home Page.**

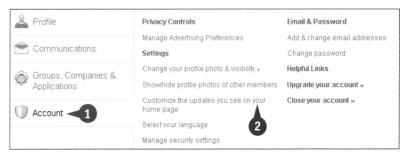

3 Review the different types of updates that appear on your home page.

4 Uncheck the box (☑ changes to ☐) for any updates that you do not want to see.

5 Click the arrow (🔽) for **How many updates do you want on your homepage** and set the number to **10, 15, 20,** or **25.**

6 Click the **Hidden** tab.

7 Click the **Show updates** button for any member whose update you hid in the past and now want to see.

8 Click the **Update type** tab.

Review your selections, and click **Save changes.**

Manage Your Security Settings

L inkedIn offers two security settings that you can adjust. One determines whether you use a secure web connection to log in to LinkedIn. The other enables two-step verification that prompts you to enter a verification code anytime you want to access LinkedIn on a new device. Both options add an extra layer of protection if security is a concern.

Manage Your Security Settings

1 At the Privacy & Settings page, make sure the **Account** tab is active.

2 Click the link to **Manage security settings.**

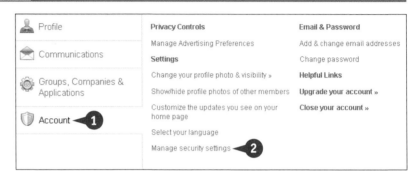

LinkedIn displays a Security Settings page with two options: **Secure connection** and **Two-step verification for sign-in.**

3 If you want to use the secure connection, check the box (☐ changes to ☑) for **A secure connection will be used when you are browsing LinkedIn.**

LinkedIn updates your security setting to use a secure connection.

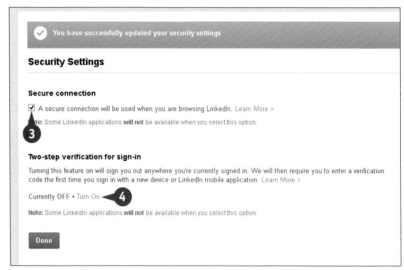

4 If you want to turn on two-step verification, click the **Turn On** link below the option.

LinkedIn displays a page asking for a phone number to use to send you the necessary verification code.

⑤ Type your mobile phone number in the **Phone Number** field.

⑥ Click the **Send Code** button.

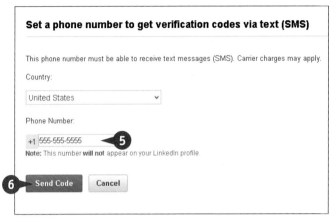

Set a phone number to get verification codes via text (SMS)

This phone number must be able to receive text messages (SMS). Carrier charges may apply.

Country:

United States

Phone Number:

+1 555-555-5555 ⑤

Note: This number **will not** appear on your LinkedIn profile.

⑥ Send Code   Cancel

LinkedIn displays a page asking you to type your verification number.

⑦ At the page, type the verification code received on your phone in the appropriate field.

⑧ Click the **Verify** button.

Turn on two-step verification

Please enter the verification code sent to ████████ [United States] and click the button below to turn on Two-Step Verification and recognize this device. Change phone number >

785358 ⑦

Didn't get it? Resend

⑧ Verify   Cancel

LinkedIn returns you to the Settings page.

⑨ Click **Done** to return to the Settings page.

Note: If you keep two-step verification turned on, you will need to request and enter a verification code anytime you log in to LinkedIn on a new device.

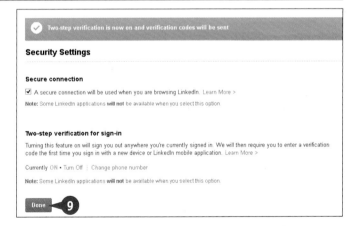

✔ Two-step verification is now on and verification codes will be sent

Security Settings

Secure connection

☑ A secure connection will be used when you are browsing LinkedIn. Learn More >

Note: Some LinkedIn applications **will not** be available when you select this option.

Two-step verification for sign-in

Turning this feature on will sign you out anywhere you're currently signed in. We will then require you to enter a verification code the first time you sign in with a new device or LinkedIn mobile application. Learn More >

Currently ON • Turn Off | Change phone number

Note: Some LinkedIn applications **will not** be available when you select this option.

Done ⑨

TIP

LinkedIn says that some LinkedIn applications will not be available when I select either of the two security options. Should I worry?

You may find that certain LinkedIn applications no longer work or display an error message when you try to access them. If so, you can easily turn off either or both of the security options. Otherwise, your normal workflow in LinkedIn will not be affected.

Change Your Password

Like any secure website, LinkedIn offers you the option to change your password at any time. To change your password, you need to know your current one before you can create a new one. Your LinkedIn password must be at least six characters in length and is case-sensitive.

Change Your Password

1. At the Privacy & Settings page, make sure the **Account** tab is active.

2. Click the link to **Change password.**

3. At the Change your password window, type your current password in the **Old password** field.

4. Type your new password in the **New password** field and again in the **Confirm new password** field.

Note: LinkedIn shows you the strength of your new password as your type it.

5. Click the **Change password** button.

    LinkedIn displays a message that your password has been changed.

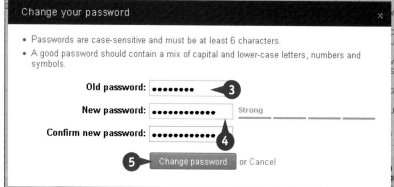

Close Your LinkedIn Account

After going through all the time and effort setting up your LinkedIn account, why would you want to close it? Well, maybe you have decided that the service is just not for you. Or maybe you discovered that you already had a LinkedIn account and want to delete one. Or maybe you just want to start fresh with a new account. Whatever the reason, LinkedIn makes it fairly easy for you to close your account.

Close Your LinkedIn Account

1 Make sure you are logged in to the account that you want to close.

2 From any LinkedIn page, hover over your thumbnail LinkedIn photo in the upper-right corner.

3 From the Accounts & Settings menu, click the **Review** link for Privacy & Settings.

4 At the Privacy & Settings page, click the **Account** tab.

5 Click the link to **Close your account.**

At the Close Account Reason page, click the button (⊙ changes to ⦿) to note the reason.

Click **Continue.**

At the Close Account Verification page, click the **Verify Account** button.

At the Close Account Consequences page. click the **Close Account**

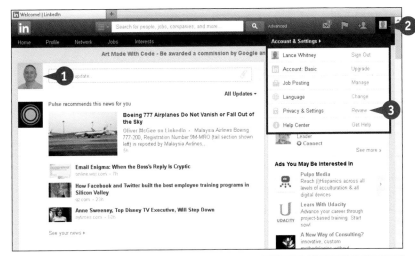

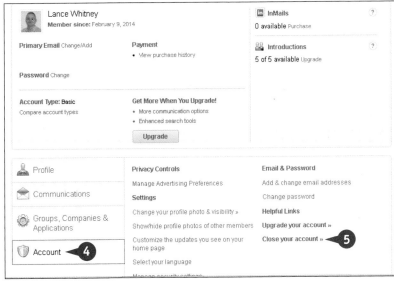

CHAPTER 13

Using LinkedIn on a Mobile Device

Yes, you can access LinkedIn on the go. Whether you own an iPhone, iPad, or Android device, you can tap into LinkedIn's dedicated mobile app and specific apps for contacts, job recruitment, and news items. You can also access LinkedIn through your device's mobile browser if no app is available.

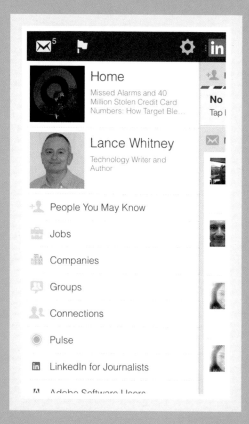

Download and Set Up LinkedIn's iPhone or iPad App

If you have an iPhone or iPad, you can download and use LinkedIn's dedicated mobile apps. These apps offer only a small subset of the features available on the full website. But they do give you the ability to post items, view recent e-mail and notifications, make new connections, run searches, and access groups. You can download the specific app directly from your iPhone or iPad.

Download and Set up LinkedIn's iPhone or iPad App

1 From your iPhone or iPad, tap the **App Store** icon.

2 In the App store, tap the search icon or field.

3 Type **LinkedIn** in the **Search** field.

The App Store displays a list of apps that match the word LinkedIn.

4 On an iPhone, tap the entry for **LinkedIn.** On an iPad, type the entry for **LinkedIn for iPad.**

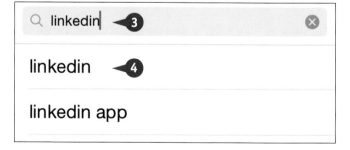

5 Tap the **FREE** button, and then tap the **INSTALL** button to download and install the app.

Your device downloads the LinkedIn mobile app and displays an **Open** button next to the app after the download has completed.

6 Tap the **OPEN** button to open the LinkedIn app.

7 Tap **Sign in.**

8 At the Sign in screen, type your LinkedIn username or e-mail in the **E-mail** field and your password in the **Password** field.

9 Tap **Sign in.**

LinkedIn displays an **Add Connections** screen, inviting you to import your address books from other sources.

10 Click the **Cancel** link to bypass this step.

LinkedIn takes you to your home page.

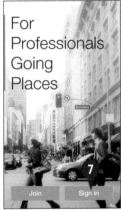

TIP

I have an iPod touch. Can I use LinkedIn's mobile app?
Yes, the iPhone version supports the iPod touch. Follow the steps in this section to download the app on your iPod touch.

Use LinkedIn's iPhone App

L inkedIn's iPhone app is fairly versatile. You can post items, view your connections, access groups, and perform other common tasks. You can also update your profile and upgrade to a premium subscription, two tasks you cannot currently do via the iPad app.

Use LinkedIn's iPhone App

1 If the LinkedIn app is closed, tap its icon on your iPhone's screen to open it.

The app displays your LinkedIn home page.

2 Scroll down to view the latest updates and comments.

3 To post an update, tap the update icon (⬛) in the upper-right corner of the screen.

4 Type your update.

5 Tap the **Visible to Anyone** link.

6 Tap either **Connections Only** or **Anyone,** depending on whom you want to see your update.

7 Tap the **Post to Twitter** button (▭ changes to ▭) if you do not want your Twitter followers to see the update.

Note: The background of the button turns from green to white after you turn it off.

8 Click the **Share** link to share your update.

LinkedIn shares your update and returns you to your home page.

9 To search for a person, job, company, or group, tap the **Search** field at the top.

10 Tap the category for the item that you seek — **People, Jobs, Companies,** or **Groups.**

11 Type your search term in the **Search** field.

LinkedIn displays a list of results that match your search term.

12 Tap any of the other three categories to see other results that match your search term.

13 Scroll through the list of search results, and tap the item you want to view.

The app displays that item.

14 Tap the back arrow (◀) to go back one screen.

15 Tap **Cancel** to exit the search results.

LinkedIn returns you to your home page.

16 Swipe your screen to the right, or tap the **LinkedIn** icon in the upper-left corner of the screen.

LinkedIn displays a screen of more features and options.

17 Tap your profile image to view your profile.

18 Scroll down to view your entire profile.

19 To update your profile, scroll to the top of the screen and tap the **Update Profile** button.

20 Scroll down your profile page, and tap the item you want to add or edit.

21 Revise the item, and then click the **Save** link at the top of the screen.

22 When you are finished updating your profile, click the **Done** link.

23 Swipe your screen to the right, or tap the **LinkedIn** icon in the upper-left corner of the screen to return to the list of features.

24 Tap each feature on the left — **People You May Know, Jobs, Companies, Groups, Connections,** and **Pulse** — to view those items. Remember to swipe to the left to return to the full list.

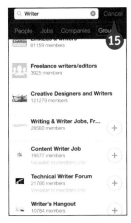

continued ▶

Use LinkedIn's iPhone App (continued)

You can access certain LinkedIn features by swiping to the right but you can also add a couple of features to the list.

25 To add more features to the list, scroll to the bottom of the list and tap the **Add shortcut** link.

26 Tap any of the items you want to add to the feature list, such as **Who's Viewed Your Profile.**

LinkedIn adds that item and returns you to the feature list.

27 Tap the Message icon (✉) at the top to see your recent invitations and e-mail messages.

28 Tap the new e-mail icon (✎) in the upper-right corner to send a new e-mail or invitation.

29 Tap either **New Message** or **New Invitation.**

30 Fill in the **To, Subject**, and message or invitation body fields, and tap **Send** to send the message.

278

LinkedIn returns you to the Invitations and Messages screen.

31 Return to the full list of features.

32 Tap the flag icon (🏴) at the top to see your latest notifications.

LinkedIn displays your latest notifications.

33 Return to the full list of features.

34 Tap the gear icon (⚙) at the top to view the settings for the LinkedIn app.

35 Tap the **Add Connections** setting if you want to add more connections by importing e-mail addresses from an external e-mail account.

36 Follow the various steps to add connections if you want.

37 Return to and review the other settings if needed.

38 Swipe the screen to the right to return to the list of features.

39 Tap the **Home** link to return to the home page.

TIP

Why do I not see all of the exact same screens in the current version of the LinkedIn app as shown here?
LinkedIn periodically updates its mobile app, so certain screens may change from time to time.

Use LinkedIn's iPad App

LinkedIn's iPad app is also fairly versatile. The iPad app is similar to the iPhone app in that you can post items, view your connections, access groups, and perform other tasks. But the layout is different, as are the steps for using certain features. Currently, you cannot update your profile or upgrade to a premium subscription on the iPad app—two tasks you can do on the iPhone version.

Use LinkedIn's iPad App

1 From your iPad, tap the **LinkedIn** icon to open the app.

2 Tap **Sign in** if required.

3 At the Sign in screen, type your LinkedIn username and password and tap **Sign in** to open the app if required.

The app displays your LinkedIn home page.

4 Scroll down to view the latest updates and comments.

5 To post an update, scroll back to the top and tap the update icon (⬚) in the upper-right corner of the screen.

6 Type your update.

7 Tap the **Share with** link.

8 Tap **Connections Only, LinkedIn + Twitter,** or **LinkedIn** depending on whom you want to see your update.

Note: Choosing the "LinkedIn" settings for sharing on the iPad app is the same as choosing "anyone" for sharing on the iPhone app.

9 Click the **Share** button to share your update.

LinkedIn shares your update.

10 To search for a person, job, company, or group, tap the **Search** field at the top.

11 Tap the category for the item that you seek, such as **Companies.**

12 Type your search term in the **Search** field.

LinkedIn displays a list of results that match your search term.

13 Tap the other categories to see other results that match your search term.

14 Tap the item you want to view.

15 Tap the **X** () in the upper-right corner of the screen to close it and return to your home page.

16 Swipe down on your screen.

17 Tap your profile image to view your profile.

18 Scroll down to view your entire profile.

19 Tap the **X** () in the upper-right corner of the screen to close it.

20 Swipe down on your screen.

21 Tap the **Connections** button to view your connections.

22 Scroll down the page, and tap a specific connection to view that person's profile.

continued ▶

You can use the LinkedIn iPad app to view your connections, your groups, and other information.

Use LinkedIn's iPad App (continued)

23 Tap the **X** (☒) in the upper-right corner of the screen to close the profile page.

24 Tap the **X** (☒) to close the connections page.

25 Again swipe down on your screen.

26 Tap the **Groups** link to view your groups.

27 Tap the group you want to view.

28 Tap the **X** (☒) to close the page for that group.

29 Tap the **X** (☒) again to close the Groups page.

30 Again swipe down on your screen.

31 Swipe the row of features to the left to view more of them, and tap any feature you want to view.

32 Tap the **X** button (❌) to close that feature's screen.

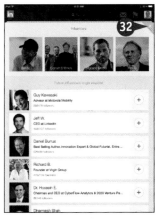

33 Swipe down on your screen, and tap the Messages icon (✉) to view your recent invitations and e-mails.

LinkedIn displays your recent invitations and e-mail messages.

34 Tap the Notifications icon (🔲) to view your recent notifications.

LinkedIn displays your recent notifications.

TIPS

Are there other features I can access through LinkedIn's iPad app?

Yes, you can access Companies, Jobs, Influencers, Channels, and more.

The top bar does not always appear. How do I view it?

Swipe down on the screen, and the top bar will appear if not already visible.

Use LinkedIn's Android App

ndroid phone or tablet owners can also tap into LinkedIn through a dedicated mobile app. The Android LinkedIn app is very similar to the iPhone app, offering virtually the same layout and same features. So you can use it to access all your LinkedIn information and to update your profile.

Use LinkedIn's Android App

1 From your Android device, tap the icon for the **Google Play** store.

2 In the Play Store, tap the Search icon at the top and type **LinkedIn** in the search field.

Google Play displays a list of suggested items.

3 Tap the **LinkedIn** item with the LinkedIn logo in front of it.

4 At the LinkedIn app page, tap the **INSTALL** button to download and install it.

5 At the App permissions window, tap the **ACCEPT** button.

Your device downloads the LinkedIn mobile app and displays an Open button next to the app after the download has completed.

6 Tap the **Open** button to open LinkedIn.

7 Tap **Sign In.**

8 At the Sign in screen, type your LinkedIn username and password in the appropriate fields and tap the **Sign In** button.

The app asks if you want to sync LinkedIn with your phone.

9 Tap the **NO, THANKS!** link.

The app then asks if you want to add connections.

10 Tap the **X** to bypass this screen.

The app displays your LinkedIn home page.

11 Scroll down to view the latest updates.

12 To post an update, tap the update icon (🔍) in the upper-right corner of the screen.

13 Type your update in the Share an update window.

14 Tap the **Visibility: Anyone** link.

15 Tap **Anyone** or **Connections only,** depending on whom you want to see your update.

Note: "Anyone" refers to anyone on LinkedIn, whether or not you are connected.

16 Tap the **Twitter** link.

17 Tap the **Don't post to Twitter** button (◉ changes to ◯) if you do not want your Twitter followers to see the update.

18 Tap the **Share** button (▶) to share your update.

19 To search for a person, job, company, or group, tap the Search icon (🔍) at the top.

20 Tap the category for the item that you seek.

21 Type your search term in the **Search** field.

22 Tap the other categories to see other results that match your search term.

23 Tap the item you want to view.

continued ▶

Using LinkedIn's Android app, you can post updates, search for people and jobs, and revise your profile, among other features.

Use LinkedIn's Android App (continued)

24 Tap the LinkedIn logo to go back one screen, and tap again to return to your home page.

25 Swipe your screen to the right, or tap the LinkedIn logo in the upper-left corner of the screen.

LinkedIn displays a screen of more features and options.

26 Tap your profile image to view your profile.

27 Scroll down to view your entire profile.

28 To update your profile, scroll to the top of the screen and tap the **Update Profile** button.

29 Scroll down your profile page, and tap the item you want to add or edit.

30 Revise the item, and click **Save.**

31 When you are finished updating your profile, tap the LinkedIn logo once and then again to return to the list of features.

32 Tap each of the features on the left — **People You May Know, Jobs, Companies, Groups, Connections**, and **Pulse** — to view each of those items. Remember to swipe to the right to return to the full list.

33 To add more features to the list, scroll to the bottom of the list and tap the **Add Shortcut** link.

34 Tap any of the items you want to add to the feature list.

The app adds the item and returns you to the feature list.

35 Tap the messaging icon (⬚) at the top to view your recent invitations and e-mail.

36 Tap the new message icon (⬚) in the upper-right corner to send a new e-mail or invitation.

37 Tap either **New Message** or **New Invitation.**

38 Fill in the **To, Subject,** and message or invitation body fields, and tap the **Send** button to send the message.

39 Tap the LinkedIn logo to return to the full list of features.

40 Tap the flag icon (⬚) at the top to see your latest notifications.

41 From the Notifications screen, tap the Settings icon (⬚) at the top to view the settings for the LinkedIn app.

42 Tap the **Add Connections** setting to add a new connection if you want the app to import e-mail addresses from an external e-mail account.

43 Tap **Continue** and follow the necessary steps to add a new connection.

 TIP

How can I return to my LinkedIn home page?
From the Settings screen, tap the Home link.

Use LinkedIn's Mobile Website

Own a mobile phone or tablet that does not offer its own dedicated app for LinkedIn? No problem. You can still access LinkedIn's website through your device's mobile browser. Depending on your device, LinkedIn will appear either as the full site just the way it appears on your computer, or as a mobile site specifically designed for a mobile device. The mobile site currently uses the same layout and format found on the iPhone and Android apps.

Use LinkedIn's Mobile Website

1 From your mobile device, open your Web browser.

Note: Depending on your device, your default mobile browser could be Safari, Firefox, Google Chrome, Opera, or even a generic browser on a basic mobile phone. You also may have installed more than one browser, in which case you can open any of them.

2 In the **browser's address** field, type **linkedin.com** and press the **Go** button or its equivalent on your device's virtual keyboard.

3 Type your LinkedIn username and password in the appropriate fields, and tap **Sign In.**

LinkedIn's website appears, either as the mobile site (touch.www.linkedin.com) or as the full site (www.linkedin.com).

4 If LinkedIn's mobile website appears, follow the steps in the section "Use LinkedIn's Android App" in this chapter to use the site, just as you would on an Android device.

5 If LinkedIn's full website appears, follow the sections and steps in Chapters **2** to **12** to use the site, just as you would on a PC.

TIP

Will I be able to access the entire range of LinkedIn's features through the mobile site?
That depends on which site appears on your mobile device. If LinkedIn's mobile website appears — touch. www.linkedin.com — then only a subset of features will be available. If the full website appears, then the entire range of features will be available.

Use the LinkedIn Contacts App

LinkedIn Contacts is an app designed to help you manage and keep in touch with all your contacts, not just those on LinkedIn. You can import contacts from other sources, view the profile information of LinkedIn members, and view alerts on their job changes and other notable events. You can also communicate with your contacts via e-mail, text message, or phone. The LinkedIn Contacts app is designed only for the iPhone, although you can run it on an iPad. But LinkedIn does not presently offer a version of this app for Android phones or tablets.

Use the LinkedIn Contacts App

1 From your iPhone, tap the **App Store** icon.

2 In the App store, tap the Search icon.

3 Type **LinkedIn Contacts** in the search field.

The App Store displays a list of apps that match the words "LinkedIn Contacts."

4 Tap the entry for **LinkedIn Contacts.**

5 Tap the **FREE** button, and then tap the **INSTALL** button to download and install the app.

Your iPhone downloads the LinkedIn mobile app and displays an **Open** button next to the app after the download has completed.

6 Tap the **Open** button to open LinkedIn Contacts.

7 At the login screen, type your LinkedIn username and password and then tap the **Sign In** button to log in to LinkedIn.

The app asks if you would like it to access your contacts.

8 If you want to manage the contacts on your iPhone through the app, tap **OK**. Otherwise, tap **Don't Allow.**

The app displays a series of four screens that explain what it does.

9 Swipe your finger to the left to see each screen.

10 Tap **Continue** to launch the app.

The app displays a list of sources for contacts that you can add to it.

11 Tap the sources (⊞ changes to ☑) that you want to add to the app.

Note: If you select an external source such as Yahoo! Mail or Gmail, LinkedIn asks you to sign in to that account.

12 In that event, type your username or e-mail address and password into the appropriate fields for your external e-mail account and tap **Sign In.**

LinkedIn asks for permission to access that account.

13 Tap **Allow access** or **Agree.**

14 At the Add sources screen, tap **Done.**

LinkedIn displays the To Do screen.

15 Tap the Contacts icon.

LinkedIn displays all your LinkedIn contacts and the contacts you added.

16 Scroll down the list of contacts, and tap a specific name that you want to view.

17 Scroll down the contact's profile to view that person's information.

18 Scroll to the top, and tap the Messaging icon (✉) to e-mail or text the person.

19 Tap the e-mail address or phone number to use for e-mail or text.

continued ▶

Through the LinkedIn Contacts app, you can communicate with one of your contacts by phone, e-mail, or text.

Use the LinkedIn Contacts App (continued)

20 Type your message in the New Message window, and tap **Send.**

21 Tap the Phone icon (📞) to call the person.

22 Tap the Note icon (📝) to add a note or reminder for that person.

Note: The app offers three options: **Add Note, Add Reminder,** and **Add How You Met.**

23 Tap the appropriate option.

24 Type the note or reminder, and then tap **Save.**

Note: You can now view that note or reminder whenever and wherever you view the person's profile.

25 Tap the **Contacts** link to return to the Contacts list.

26 Tap the **Filters** link.

27 Tap one of the options in the Sort By section to sort the contact list by one of three filters: **Alphabetical, Recent Conversation,** or **Newly Added.**

The app displays your contacts according to the filter.

28 Tap the **Filters** link again.

29 Tap one of the options in the Filter By section to filter the contact list by **Tags, Companies, Titles, Locations,** or **Sources.**

30 Tap a specific criterion for the category you selected.

The app displays the contact list to show only the people who match the filter you selected.

31 Tap the link for the category name at the top to return to the Filters screen.

32 Tap the **Filters** link.

33 Tap one of the options in the Sort By section to display all your contacts again.

34 Tap the **To Do** icon to see a list of to-do items for your contacts.

35 Tap a specific item to complete it.

36 Type a comment, and tap the **Comment** link.

The app removes the item from the list.

37 Swipe a specific to-do item to the left to dismiss it.

TIP

I have an iPod touch. Can I use the LinkedIn Contacts app?
Yes, the iPhone version supports the iPod touch. Follow the steps in this section to download and install the app on your iPod touch.

Use the LinkedIn Pulse App

LinkedIn Pulse is a dedicated mobile app for LinkedIn's Pulse news service. As described in the "Use LinkedIn Pulse" section in Chapter 10, LinkedIn Pulse offers news stories and other items of interest. The Pulse app is a news reader that serves up all the latest news items from your favorite categories and channels in one single mobile spot. The app is available for the iPhone, iPad, and Android devices.

Use the LinkedIn Pulse App

1 From your iPhone or iPad, open the App Store. From your Android device, open Google Play.

2 In the mobile store app, tap the **Search** icon or field.

3 Type **linkedIn pulse** in the search field.

The mobile store displays a list of apps that match the phrase "LinkedIn Pulse."

4 Tap the entry for **LinkedIn Pulse.**

5 Tap the appropriate button to download and install the app.

Your device downloads the LinkedIn Pulse app and displays an **Open** button next to the app after the download has completed.

6 Tap the **Open** button to open LinkedIn Pulse.

7 At the login screen, type your LinkedIn username and password and tap the **Sign In With LinkedIn** button to log in to LinkedIn and open the app.

The app brings you directly to the All Channels page.

8 Tap a news story that you want to read.

9 Tap the Back button () on an iPhone or iPad to return to the main All Channels screen.

10 To find more channels to follow, scroll to the bottom of the screen and tap the **Find more to follow!** button.

11 Tap a category that interests you.

12 In that category, tap the plus button (⊞ changes to ⊘) of a channel you want to follow.

The app displays a check mark next to that channel.

13 To return to the previous screen, tap the back arrow.

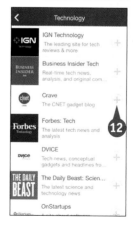

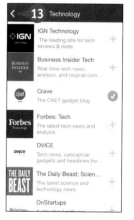

continued ▶

With the LinkedIn Pulse app, you can add and view different channels to keep up with the latest news from your favorite sources.

Use the LinkedIn Pulse App (continued)

14 To search for a specific source, tap the **Search** icon at the top of the screen.

15 Type the name of the source or topic that you want to find in the **Search** field.

16 Tap the name of the source you want to follow from the list of suggestions.

17 Tap the plus icon (⊕ changes to ✓) in the top-right corner to add that source to your All Channels list.

The app adds a check mark to that channel.

18 Tap the back arrow to return to the search results screen.

19 At the search results screen, tap **Done** to return to the list of categories.

20 Tap **Done** again to return to your All Channels page.

21 Swipe your finger down the screen to move to the top of the All Channels screen if you are not already there.

22 To manage your channels, tap the **Edit** link.

The app displays all your channels.

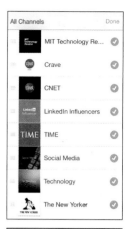

23 To move a channel higher or lower in the list, hold down the three-line icon in front of the channel logo and drag the channel up or down the page. Release the channel when it is in the desired spot.

24 To remove a channel from your all Channels list, tap the check mark icon ().

The app asks if you want to delete the channel.

25 Tap **Delete.**

26 Tap the **Done** link to return to your All Channels page.

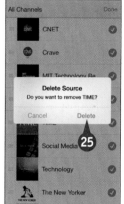

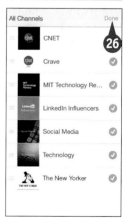

TIP

What categories of news stories can I access through LinkedIn Pulse?
You can access stories across a variety of categories, including general news, technology, business, science, politics, lifestyle, art & design, photography, entertainment, sports, inspiration, food, fun & humor, and gaming.

CHAPTER 14

Using LinkedIn with Other Sites and Services

LinkedIn can play nicely with other websites and services. Specifically, you can share online articles and other web pages directly on LinkedIn and access certain LinkedIn features through toolbars for your browser.

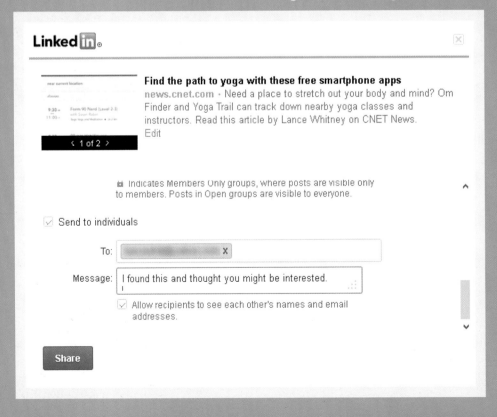

Share a Web Page via LinkedIn

Find an article or web page that you would like to share with your LinkedIn connections? No problem. The "Post Your Own Updates" section in Chapter 4 explains how you can copy and paste a web page's URL into a LinkedIn post. But many web pages offer a dedicated LinkedIn Share button that you can click to share that page on LinkedIn. Clicking that button displays a small form that you can fill out to easily share the page.

Share a Web Page via LinkedIn

1 At the web page you want to share, click the LinkedIn **Share** button.

Note: You can spot the **Share** button because it displays the familiar LinkedIn logo.

The page displays the Share news on LinkedIn form.

2 Type something in the text box if you want to comment on the page.

3 Click the **Share with: Public** down arrow (⌄).

4 Select **Connections** if you want to share the page only with the people in your immediate network.

5 Click the **Twitter** check box (☐ changes to ☑) if you want to share the page with your Twitter followers.

6 To share the page as an update in one of your groups, click the **Post to groups** check box (☐ changes to ☑).

7 In the **Group(s)** field, type and select the name of the group with which you want to share the page.

Note: You can share the page with more than one group by typing and selecting the names of additional groups.

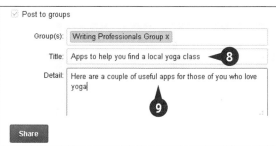

8 In the **Title** field, type a title for the discussion that you want to start.

9 In the **Detail** field, type any further comments you want to make on this page for the group discussion.

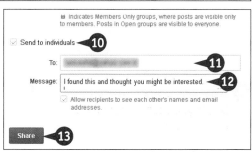

10 Scroll down, and click the **Send to individuals** check box (☐ changes to ☑) if you want to share the page with certain people via e-mail.

11 In the **To** field, type the name or e-mail address of the person with whom you want to share the page.

12 Then type a personal message if needed.

13 Click the **Share** button to share the page.

LinkedIn flashes a message telling you that you have successfully shared the page.

14 Click **Close** to close the LinkedIn sharing form.

I do not see the LinkedIn Share button on a particular page. Where can I find it?
Not all web pages display the LinkedIn Share button. If you do not see it right away, look for and click the **More** link next to the icons for other social network sites to see if the LinkedIn Share button appears.

Use the LinkedIn Sharing Bookmarklet

You stumble across a web page that you want to share on LinkedIn, but no Share button is available. Can you still share the page without having to copy and paste its URL into a LinkedIn post? Yes, you can do just that through LinkedIn's Sharing Bookmarklet. This type of bookmark generates the Share form that was covered in the preceding section.

Use the LinkedIn Sharing Bookmarklet

1 From your browser, open the following web page: https://www.linkedin.com/static?key=browser_bookmarklet.

Your browser opens LinkedIn's Sharing Bookmarklet page.

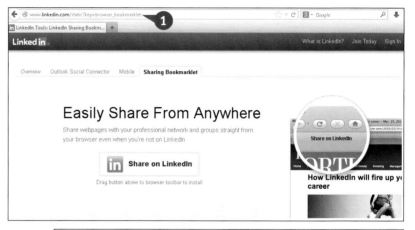

2 If you are using Firefox, and your browser does not already display the Bookmarks Toolbar, right-click anywhere in the top space of the browser next to the plus symbol. If you are using Internet Explorer, skip to step **5**.

3 From the pop-up menu in Firefox, click the **Bookmarks Toolbar** option.

4 Drag the large **Share on LinkedIn** button, and drop it in onto your Bookmarks toolbar.

You should now see a **Share on LinkedIn** button on the Bookmarks toolbar.

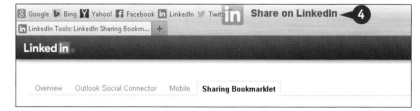

⑤ If you are using Internet Explorer and your browser does not already display the Favorites bar, right-click anywhere in the top space of the browser.

⑥ From the pop-up menu, click the **Favorites bar** option.

The Favorites bar appears.

⑦ Right-click the large **Share on LinkedIn** button.

⑧ From the popup menu, click the **Add to favorites** option.

⑨ In the Add a Favorite window, click the **Create in:** down arrow and change the location to **Favorites.**

⑩ Click **Add**.

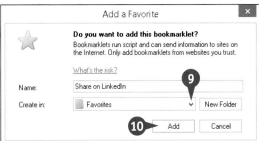

You should now see a **Share on LinkedIn** button on the Favorites bar.

⑪ For either Internet Explorer or Firefox, open the web page that you want to share.

⑫ Click the **Share on LinkedIn** button.

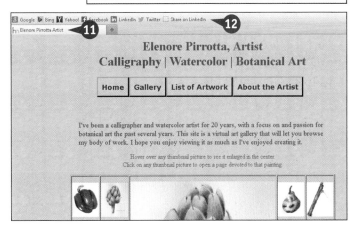

If you have not already logged in to LinkedIn through this browser on this computer before, then you will receive a prompt to sign into your account.

In that event, type your LinkedIn username and password and click the **Sign in** button to sign into LinkedIn.

The page you want to share then displays the Share news on LinkedIn form.

Follow steps **2** through **13** in the previous section to share the page.

TIP

Can I share any web page through the bookmarklet?
Yes, you can share any web page using this process.

Use the LinkedIn Browser Toolbar

Does LinkedIn offer another way to tap into its different features without having to directly navigate the website? Yes, through a browser toolbar. Available for both Internet Explorer and Firefox, the LinkedIn Browser Toolbar gives you access to certain pages and features on LinkedIn and offers a handy search tool to track down jobs, companies, and other items listed on the site.

Use the LinkedIn Browser Toolbar

1 From your browser, open the following web page: https://www.linkedin.com/static?key=ie_toolbar_download_promo.

2 If you are using Firefox, click the **Download It Now** button for Firefox Toolbar 3.3. If you are using Internet Explorer, skip to step **8**.

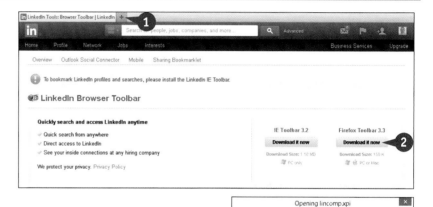

3 At the Opening lincomp.xpi window, make sure the **Save File** button is the active button and then click **OK.**

4 Click the **Download** arrow to view the downloaded lincomp.xpi file.

5 Drag the lincomp.xpi file anywhere onto your Firefox window.

6 At the Software Installation window, wait a couple of seconds for the **Install Now** button to be enabled and then click that button.

A message pops up telling you that LinkedIn Companion for Firefox will be installed after you restart Firefox.

7 Click the **Restart Now** button.

Firefox restarts and displays a page telling you that LinkedIn Companion for Firefox is now installed on your browser.

8 In Internet Explorer, click the **Download it now** link for IE Toolbar 3.2.

9 At the File Download window, click the **Run** button to install the toolbar.

10 If you receive a User Account Control message, click **Yes** to allow the following program to make changes to this computer.

The program displays the LinkedIn Internet Explorer Toolbar Setup Wizard.

continued ▶

Use the LinkedIn Browser Toolbar (continued)

11 Click **Next** to start the wizard.

12 At the License Agreement window, click the check box for **I accept the terms of the License Agreement** and then click the **Next** button.

13 At the Choose Install Location window, click the **Install** button.

14 If the program displays a message saying that you need to close all Internet Explorer and Windows Explorer windows, click **Yes.**

The installation kicks off.

15 At the Completing the LinkedIn Internet Explorer Toolbar Setup Wizard window, make sure the check box for **Launch Internet Explorer with LinkedIn Toolbar** is checked. Click the **Finish** button.

16 If you receive a message saying that the LinkedIn Toolbar is ready for use, click the **Enable** button to turn it on.

Internet Explorer then displays the LinkedIn Toolbar.

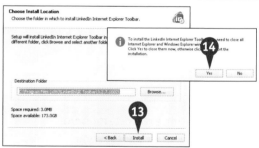

Note: In Firefox, the LinkedIn Toolbar appears as a single menu with multiple commands. In Internet Explorer, the toolbar displays multiple features in a single row. The two are similar, though the IE toolbar offers a dedicated search tool.

17 In Firefox, click the **LinkedIn** menu on the toolbar and click each feature in the menu to try them all.

18 In Internet Explorer, click the down arrow next to the LinkedIn button on the toolbar and click each feature in the menu to try them all.

19 In Internet Explorer, click the Search arrow (🔽) and select a category in which you want to search.

20 In the **Enter search term here** field, type the item that you want to find and press Enter (or Return) on your keyboard.

LinkedIn opens to display a list of results in response to your search.

Note: The toolbars for both Firefox and Internet Explorer also offer a **Share on/in LinkedIn** button, which works exactly like the LinkedIn Sharing Bookmarklet discussed in the preceding section.

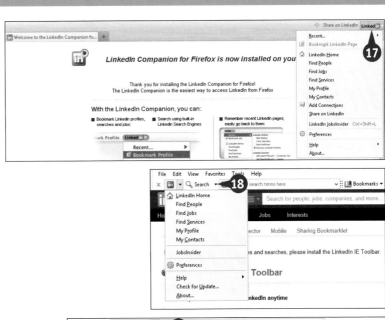

TIP

Why would I use the Browser Toolbar instead of the regular LinkedIn website?
The Browser Toolbar offers several of LinkedIn's key features in one easily-accessible and convenient place.

CHAPTER 15

Getting Help and Advice on LinkedIn

Where can you turn if you have questions or problems on LinkedIn? The site offers its own help center and forum through which you can search for information and post questions. You can also contact LinkedIn directly with comments and concerns. And you can follow LinkedIn on Facebook and Twitter to stay abreast of the site's latest news and developments.

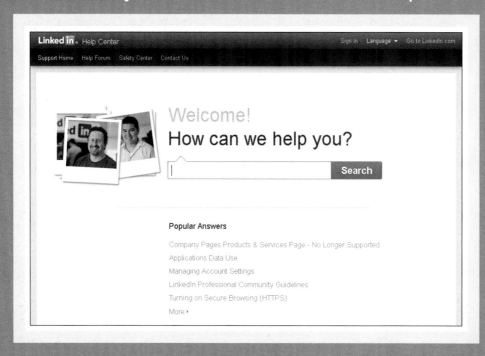

Use LinkedIn's Help Center

LinkedIn's Help Center provides a wealth of information on all the site's features. You can browse the Help Center to see an overview of general topics. Or you can search for a specific item to learn what it does and how to use it.

Use LinkedIn's Help Center

1 From any LinkedIn page, hover over your profile photo and click the **Get Help** link for the Help Center.

LinkedIn opens a web page for the Help Center site where you can browse for information or type a specific question.

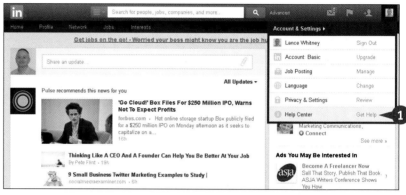

2 Click one of the categories under Popular Answers to browse for information on a particular topic, such as **Managing Account Settings.**

LinkedIn displays a page with information and links on that topic.

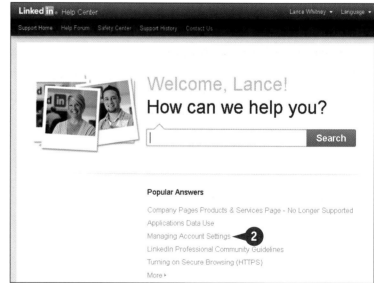

3 Click a link for a subtopic that interests you.

LinkedIn displays a page with information on that subtopic.

4 Click the **Support Home** link to return to the Help Center's home page.

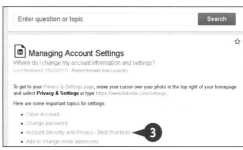

5 If you have a specific question or problem related to LinkedIn, type your query in the search field.

6 Click the **Search** button.

LinkedIn displays a page with links to answers that may address your question.

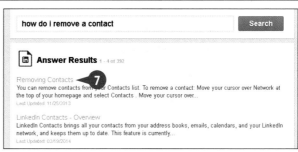

7 Click the link that best answers your question.

8 If you want, you can click **Yes** or **No** at the bottom to tell LinkedIn whether the answer was helpful.

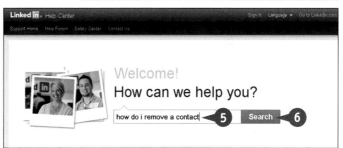

9 Click the **Support Home** link to return to the Help Center's home page.

LinkedIn returns you to the Support Home page.

TIP

How should I phrase my search query?
You can phrase it as a question or statement, but make sure to include all of the keywords that describe your *topic*.

Use LinkedIn's Help Forum

Having trouble finding the answers or information you seek through the Help Center? You may want to try LinkedIn's Help Forum. This discussion forum consists of questions and answers from fellow LinkedIn members. You can search the forum to see if your question has already been answered. If not, you can pose your question as a new discussion where it can potentially pick up an answer from someone else on LinkedIn.

Use LinkedIn's Help Forum

1 From LinkedIn's Help Center, click the link for the **Help Forum.**

LinkedIn displays the Help Forum site with a list of recent questions.

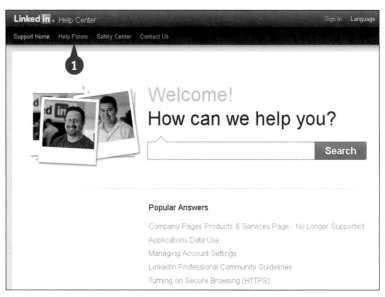

2 Click a question that interests you.

LinkedIn displays the full question and any responses.

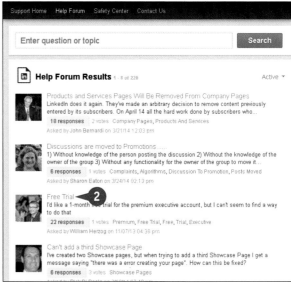

3 To search for a specific discussion, type a question or problem in the search field at the top of the page.

4 Click the **Search** button.

LinkedIn displays results related to your question.

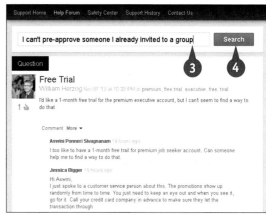

5 Scroll down the response page to the Help Forum Results section.

6 Click a question or comment that most closely matches your own.

LinkedIn displays the question along with any responses to it from other members.

7 To post a new question, click the **Start a discussion** link at the top of the page.

8 At the Start a Discussion form, type the basic question in a single line in the **Your Question** field.

9 Add more details to your question in the **More details** field.

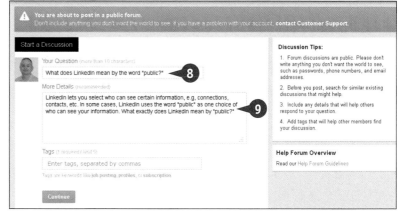

continued ▶

At LinkedIn's Help Forum, you can search for prior questions and answers or post your own question.

Use LinkedIn's Help Forum (continued)

10 Type at least one topic related to your question in the **Tags** field.

11 Click the appropriate tag from LinkedIn's list of suggestions, or click in the **Tags** field to use your tag.

12 Click **Continue.**

LinkedIn displays a Start a discussion message so you can review your question.

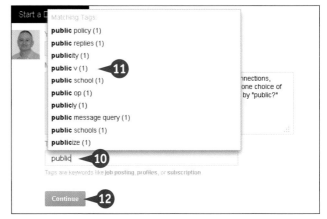

13 Click the **Edit Discussion** button to revise your post, or click **Post Discussion** to post it.

LinkedIn posts and displays your question.

Note: By default, you will see any response to your question as a message in your primary e-mail account, but you can directly view your question and any responses on the site.

14 To see your discussions, hover over the **Help Forum** button and click **Your Discussions.**

LinkedIn tells you how many responses your post has received.

15 Click the link for your question to view the responses.

LinkedIn displays the responses.

16 Click the Comment link to reply to the response.

17 Type your comment in the comment field.

18 Click the **Comment** button.

19 Notice that LinkedIn adds your comment to the discussion.

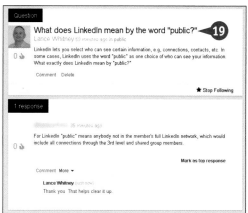

TIP

Can I respond to questions from other LinkedIn members?

Yes, if you believe you know the answer to a question, you can add your own response.

Use LinkedIn's Safety Center

Concerned about maintaining your security and privacy on LinkedIn and on the Internet in general? The site's Safety Center offers advice on how to safeguard your online identity, protect yourself against malware and spam, and report inappropriate messages and other content that you receive on LinkedIn.

Use LinkedIn's Safety Center

1. From LinkedIn's Help Center, click the link for the **Safety Center.**

LinkedIn displays the Safety Center site.

2. Scroll down to the Family Center section, and click the link for **Teens.**

   LinkedIn displays information for teenagers who use the site.

3. At the top of the page, click the link for **Parents & educators.**

   LinkedIn displays information for adults who have teenagers or students with accounts on LinkedIn.

④ At the top of the page, click the link for **Law enforcement.**

LinkedIn displays information to explain how the site works with law enforcement officials.

⑤ At the top of the page, click the link for **Safety Center** to return to the main page.

⑥ Scroll down to the Privacy & Identity section, and click the link for **Protecting your identity.**

LinkedIn displays information on how to protect your online identity.

⑦ Click each of the other links at the top one by one — **Protecting your account, Protecting your privacy,** and **Your profile name** — to read information on protecting your LinkedIn account and profile.

⑧ After you have reviewed the information in the Privacy & Identify section, move to the **Security Tips** section and click each of the links one by one — **Phishing, Spam messages, Security vulnerabilities, Malware and viruses,** and **Security products** — to learn how to protect yourself against malware, viruses, spam, and other online threats.

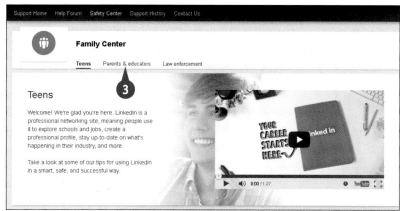

TIP

Is there a way to report a safety or security concern on LinkedIn?
Yes, scroll to the bottom of the Safety Center page and click the **Reporting a Problem** link.

Contact LinkedIn

Unable to get answers to a question from the Help Center or Help Forum? Then it may be time to turn to LinkedIn itself. You can contact LinkedIn support with a specific question or problem. Contacting support directly is often the best option if you are having trouble with your own account or profile and may not want to share the details publicly through the Help Forum.

Contact LinkedIn

1 From LinkedIn's Help Center, click the link to **Contact Us.**

LinkedIn displays a Submit Your Question form.

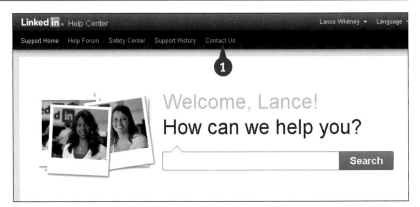

2 In the **Name** field, type your first and last name.

3 In the **Primary E-mail** field, type your e-mail address.

4 In the **Alternate E-mail** field, type any alternate e-mail address that you want to receive the response to your question.

5 In the **Issue Type** field, click the down arrow (⌄) and select the issue that best describes your question or problem.

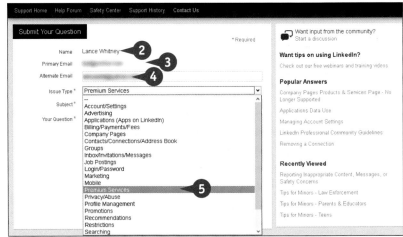

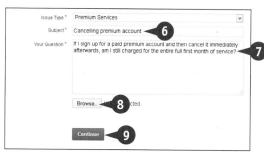

6 In the **Subject** field, type the subject of your question.

7 In the **Your Question** field, type the actual question.

8 If you need to upload a file related to your question, click the **Browse** button and double-click the file to add to your question.

Note: If you are running into a specific error on LinkedIn, you can create a screenshot of the error message and upload that image to your question.

9 Click **Continue.**

LinkedIn displays a message telling you that your question hasn't been submitted yet and suggests some possible answers.

10 Click any of the links displayed in the message if you think one of them might answer your question.

11 Click the **Edit Question** link if you want to revise your question.

12 Otherwise, click the **Submit** button.

LinkedIn submits your question and displays a support ticket that you can review, update, or close.

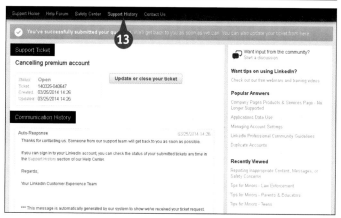

13 To view your support ticket at any point, click the **Support History** link.

LinkedIn displays a history of all your support tickets.

14 Click the ticket you want to view.

LinkedIn displays that ticket.

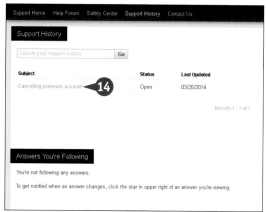

TIP

How will I know if my question has been answered?
You can always check your support history, but you will also receive a direct response to your ticket by e-mail.

View LinkedIn Webinars and Training Videos

Another way to learn about LinkedIn is through webinars and video tutorials. LinkedIn offers live and recorded webinars on a small but helpful range of topics. You can view training videos on the basics of LinkedIn, looking for a job, creating a company page, and using a premium account, among other items.

View LinkedIn Webinars and Training Videos

1 From LinkedIn's Help Center, click the link for the **Help Forum.**

2 At the Help Forum page, click the link to **Check out our free webinars and training videos.**

LinkedIn displays a list of current training videos, some of which are available as pre-recorded sessions and others that are available live.

3 Click the link to view a pre-recorded video.

LinkedIn opens a separate tab or page in your browser and displays the pre-recorded video via YouTube.

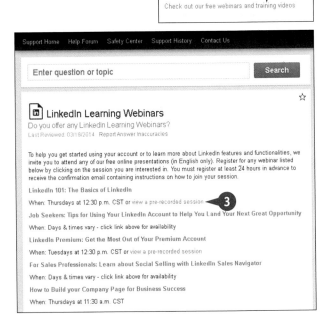

4 At the YouTube page, you can pause and restart the video, change the volume, and switch between the smaller viewing window and full screen.

The page also displays related links to other YouTube videos on LinkedIn.

5 Click another recorded video to view it.

6 Close the YouTube page to return to LinkedIn's list of training videos.

7 Click the title of a webinar that you want to view live.

LinkedIn displays a registration form for the video.

8 Select a date for the webinar you want to attend.

9 Type your first and last name and e-mail address in the appropriate fields.

10 Click the **Register** button to submit your registration.

LinkedIn confirms your registration. You also will receive a confirmation e-mail with the details on the live webinar.

Note: Certain webinars offer different types of registration forms, but the overall process remains the same.

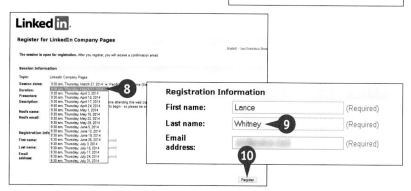

How do I attend a live LinkedIn webinar?
Click the link to the webinar in your confirmation e-mail at the scheduled time. Click the **Join Now** button to join the webinar. Note that you may be asked to install special software to view the webinar.

View the LinkedIn Blog

You can stay abreast of the latest developments with LinkedIn by checking out the site's own official blog. The LinkedIn blog culls news, stories, and other items of interest from its sites into one section. You can browse the entire lineup of blog posts from recent to older ones or search the blog site for a particular topic.

View the LinkedIn Blog

1 Move to the bottom of your profile page.

2 Click the **Blog** link.

LinkedIn displays its blog page with links to the most recent posts.

3 Click a post you want to read.

4 After reading the post, click the link to **Popular Posts** at the top of the page. On smaller resolution screens, you may need to click a three bar icon (≡) at the top of the page to display the link for **Popular Posts.**

5 On the smaller resolution screen, click the link for **Popular Posts.**

6 At the Popular Posts page, click a post you want to read.

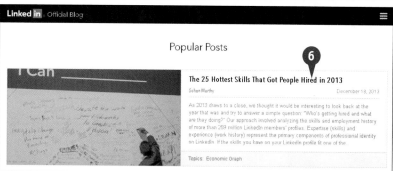

7 Click the **Topics** link at the top of the page. Again, on smaller resolution screens, you may need to click the three bar icon (▤) first and then click the **Topics** link.

8 At the Topics page, click a topic that interests you.

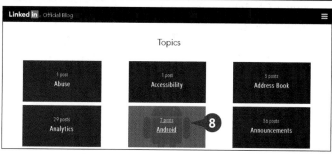

9 Click a post in that topic area that you want to read.

10 Click the **Official Blog** link at the top of the page to return to the blog's home page.

Follow LinkedIn on Facebook and Twitter

LinkedIn has its own pages on Facebook and Twitter that you can follow to keep abreast of the latest news and information from the site. The posts on both Facebook and Twitter offer links to helpful articles, advice, and other topics of interest to LinkedIn users.

Follow LinkedIn on Facebook and Twitter

Follow LinkedIn on Facebook

1 Open your web browser, and log in to your Facebook account at www.facebook.com.

2 Type **linkedin** in the Search field at the top of the page.

3 Click the entry for **LinkedIn** among the suggested search results.

Facebook displays LinkedIn's page.

4 Scroll down LinkedIn's page to view the different posts.

5 Click the link for a post you want to read.

Facebook opens the full story in LinkedIn in a separate browser tab or page.

Close the tab or page for the story to return to LinkedIn's Facebook page.

6 Scroll to the top of LinkedIn's Facebook page.

7 Click the **Like** button to like LinkedIn's Facebook page.

LinkedIn shows that you have liked the page.

Note: By liking the page, you also are now automatically following it so that updates from the page will appear in your own Facebook news feed.

Follow LinkedIn on Twitter

1 Open the Twitter website, and log into your Twitter account at www. twitter.com.

2 Type **linkedin** in the Search field at the top of the page.

3 Click the entry for **LinkedIn** among the suggested search results.

Twitter displays LinkedIn's feed.

4 Scroll down LinkedIn's Twitter feed to view the different tweets.

5 Click the link for a story you want to read.

LinkedIn opens the full story in a separate browser tab or page.

Close the separate tab or page to return to LinkedIn's Twitter feed page.

6 Scroll to the top of the page.

7 Click the **Follow** button to follow LinkedIn's Twitter feed.

Twitter indicates that you are now following this account.

Note: Following an account on Twitter displays its tweets on your own Twitter timeline.

Index